PEOPLE NEED PEOPLE

PEOPLE NEED PEOPLE

By

Samuel Southard

THE WESTMINSTER PRESS
Philadelphia

STANDARD BOOK NO. 664–24871–3

LIBRARY OF CONGRESS CATALOG CARD NO. 71–91878

Published by The Westminster Press ®
Philadelphia, Pennsylvania

To
Frances, Pamela, and Melanie

Contents

Introduction

People Need People

"People who need people are the luckiest people in the world." So Fanny Brice sings in *Funny Girl.* It is a song of dependency. Lovers lean on each other. Parents look for children's love. Children depend on parents. Husbands and wives sustain each other.

These are the lucky people. At least it seems that way to an independent, aggressive girl who is lonely for love. How wonderful it would be to depend on a man!

But the song of Fanny Brice may sound funny to many of us. Isn't she joking? "Dependency" is a degrading word in our society. We don't like to think of ourselves as people who really need anybody. We can take care of ourselves, make our own way, pull our own weight.

I wonder if we are really as self-sufficient as "self-made men" would have us believe. The man who climbs all alone to the top may also be the individual who drinks too much to drown memories and loneliness. The woman who proclaims that she doesn't need anyone may become so cold and hard inside that she can't even live with herself.

Maybe we should recognize another side of ourselves, the part that cries out for security, affection, the desire to be needed. Until we see and secure that side of life, we are incomplete persons. The "lucky" ones are those who have a balance of dependence and independence.

Of course, some people need no reminders of their dependent needs. They are continual losers, droopers, flat tires on the bandwagon. In fact, they are so painfully aware of their desire to please others that they degrade themselves without ceasing. I would like to say a few good things about these "yea-sayers" in this book. They may have more in themselves than they can admit.

Understanding words about dependent people may also do good to those who are independent. The self-reliant person has trouble with wallflowers. He is frustrated by those who disappear into the woodwork when he wants them to stand up and answer for themselves. Perhaps my analysis of the dependent personality will increase the autonomous individual's ability to live with those who live for his approval.

And the autonomous person may suddenly find that *he* has become dependent. Illness, misfortune, tragedy, can come upon healthy, happy, and successful people. At such a time the person who has recognized and accepted his need for security is lucky. He knows how to depend on others when he has to. People who know that they need people are the smartest people in the world.

Chapter 1

No Hiding Place

The World That Was

The refrain of a Negro spiritual is, "There is no hiding place down here." It is a song about the Last Judgment and the inability of sinners to find a cave in which they may hide from an angry God. The refrain is also a haunting reminder of the problem before many middle-class white Americans. In the midst of an affluent society, people are still looking for a hiding place.

There was a time when we could hide "down here." There were established shelters in family, class, occupation, religion, and state. So long as a man stayed in his place, he was secure. For example, in 1860 Robert E. Lee was leaving his army post in Texas for a return to his native Virginia. An officer in the newly created Confederate Army demanded that all federal arms and supplies be taken from him. Colonel Lee indignantly replied that he was an officer and a Virginian. He did not take orders from Texans.

This is only one of many, many stories told about the decisiveness of Lee. He had the security of a place—Virginia, with which he completely identified.

How old-fashioned that story sounds today! The stable

society of our grandparents is gone. Two world wars and a depression have undermined the nineteenth-century stability.

In the 1920's, poets and novelists wrote of a "lost generation." These were the young people who went to France during and after World War I and assumed that when they returned to the United States, it would be the same. But it was not the generation that was lost, it was the world out of which that generation came. The shock of that recognition produced works such as *The Waste Land* and *Ulysses*. To James Joyce, it seemed that the bottom had fallen out of the historical tradition. Who would build up a new form of hope in a land in which the old images had collapsed?

Rebuilding calls for independence, and independence seems to have belonged to a long-forgotten generation. There were self-confident men like John Adams and Thomas Jefferson, who felt themselves capable of building a new kind of republic, and did. There were Puritan fathers like Increase Mather and Cotton Mather, who sat in their studies and consulted God alone about matters of state.

But can men be trusted to think for themselves today? After all, we have obligations that previous generations did not dream of. Consider the $400 billion installment debt of the American householder. The business and finance section of *The Washington Post,* May 7, 1967, warned that "a lot of people might be getting in over their heads." Daily there is a heavier debt for homes, automobiles, TV sets, washing machines, and refrigerators.

Who can be "independent" with a $15,000 mortgage and a $2,000 overdraft at the bank that is called "easy credit"? If a man disagreed with his boss today, and was told to "resign," how would he meet the installment payments that take almost half of his next paycheck?

In order that we may hold on to what we have, we

fight for security rather than independence. The guaranteed annual wage is one answer to installment buying for workmen. In a job, the white-collar employee looks for the additional benefits of life insurance, health insurance, pension plans, and tenure. And beyond the large corporation, we look to the Government for social security, unemployment compensation, and medical assistance.

Despising the Dependent

We are searching for new sources of security in society. A poignant illustration of this is the plight of "twenty-year men" in the armed services. Many of these men retire with a pension by age forty and look for a new civilian life. There can be severe adjustment problems for the career officer or enlisted personnel. They had grown completely accustomed to maintenance. Decisions about quarters, food, clothes, travel, behavior, duties, had been made for them.

The sudden removal of all those supports calls for radical adjustment. Some men are confused, some are depressed, some reenlist. There are others who enjoy their retirement or who find new fulfillment in civilian occupations. But it's difficult. American society does not yet offer the built-in security that a highly organized military establishment can provide.

Of course, in civilian life it seems safer to stay where things are secure. If a man ventures out into new occupations, he is considered brave indeed. And if a person thinks independent thoughts, there will be "criticism." There can be plenty of criticism for those who reject the established policy of powerful institutions. A former White House aide, Richard N. Goodwin, described the reaction of his associates to dissenters. If Senator Fulbright challenged foreign policy, there were immediate mutterings that he was a "bad" Foreign Relations Committee chairman. Senator Wayne Morse was described as a "wild man." If intellectuals disagreed with White House policy, they were thought to be cowardly, or alienated, or unkind to Texans.[1]

In the midst of such a barrage, many people feel like a character in Damon Runyon's story of a gang war. A little gambler saw that two mobs were hunting each other for the kill, and that the police would probably be hunting everyone around them when the smoke had cleared. The gambler tried to think of a safe place where he could go for the evening, where people would be sure to remember he had been there and testify on his behalf.

There are places where we can go. But what do we think of ourselves when we have found social security? If we find refuge in a large corporation, we may find ourselves little more than "organization men." If we are successful in a profession, we may conform so much that we are accused of being "men in gray flannel suits." Or if we flee from the problems of the inner city to the quietness of the suburbs, we are just a part of "the mackerel plaza," or "the split-level fellowship."

These are the popular titles with which sociologists relentlessly chart our continuous conformity. It may make us feel like the refugees whom Trutz Rendtorff described in Germany. He found that refugees from the East collected in the Western churches each Sunday. Here were people who had not been reintegrated into society, single women and recipients of pensions, the socially weaker who were not able to adjust to the new environment. The established members of the community, with strong roots in the past, very rarely were to be found in church on Sunday.[2]

Psychologists also seem to think that we are in bad shape when we conform. Erich Fromm writes: "Every means of protecting himself from anxiety by accepting standards imposed upon him, from father, society, state, arbitrary God, is in fact a way of destroying his potential for productivity."[3]

Fromm has indicated almost every traditional—and present—source of security! He certainly has issued some powerful warnings against the desire to abandon individuality and freedom in order to overcome the experience of aloneness and powerlessness in a complicated world. He has laid bare the devastating character effects of a struggle for success in which one is constantly in need of confirmation by others.

Fromm is especially perceptive in his analysis of authority. He describes rational authority as a competence that wins respect for self and from others. In specific tasks under competent leadership, the interests of people are not antagonistic, but complementary. Rational authority provokes elements of love, admiration, or gratitude. One may want to identify partially or wholly with the leader.

But there is also an irrational authority that rests on force or cunning. Its purpose is exploitation. The boss, or leader, wants to perpetuate the relationship with those subjected to him. The result is antagonism. The helpless worker or group member must cover up his anger against the authority who exploits him.

Why do some people want this irrational authority? It is the expression of an underlying conflict between desires to be independent and strong and desires to submerge oneself in the world. Without a satisfying background of love and support from parents and other powerful figures, a man can decide that he will gain security through manipulative power. He despises the powerless, whom he delights in embarrassing. He humiliates and dominates those over whom he has control. Thus, he thinks that he is secure. At the same time, the loveless authority submits to those who are more powerful than he is. There is great admiration for those who could hurt him, and great contempt for those whom he can hurt.

Such a person is still living in the world of a hurt child. He thinks as an adult that he is really as helpless as he was in early childhood. The world is an unfriendly place and anyone who does not submit to him is an enemy.

These are the authorities that make us despise ourselves when we submit to them. There are times when we must comply with their demands because we have no alternative at that time. But, when possible, we escape or gain power in healthy ways to resist these loveless individuals.

There is a difference between compliance for survival under special social circumstances and conformity as a state of mind. Conformity is a loss of independence, an inability to distinguish information from source, an unconscious feeling that we must immediately agree with any powerful person. A conformist changes his mind automatically to be on the side of the nearest person who is powerful.

An independent person may comply with a particular demand, but he considers the source, the issue, and the situation.

Complying Without Conforming

Some people may be judging themselves too harshly when they say, "I am dependent." They may be confusing conformity with compliance. It is possible to socialize and adjust without necessarily losing one's independence.

The problem of dependency is more human and hopeful than some of us might imagine. The basic issue is balance. How do we keep a relationship between our strivings for independence and our need to depend on other people and society? Or how do we do what we want to do and still have some regard for the feelings of others and the customs of our culture?

There really should be no sharp division between our desire for approval and our self-affirmation. People in human association wish to preserve their self-esteem and simultaneously to have warm relations with their fellows.

We have been misled both by our society and by some popular psychological teachings into the belief that any dependence upon others is an automatic loss of individuality. Gordon Allport, of the psychology department at Harvard University, pointed to one reason for this. He noted in *Personality and Social Encounter* that many psychologists had sidestepped any serious study of the human desire for love and affection. The tender relationships of life were disregarded and most emphasis was placed on discord, hostility, sexual conflict.

In this "flight from tenderness," psychologists missed the importance of the giving and receiving of affection.

Allport pictures the strength of this motivation in research on the combat motivation of soldiers in World War II. Even under extreme stress, twice as many men held to their task because of affection and concern for their comrades, rather than from a motive of hatred for the enemy. The common explanation was that men did not want to let each other down.

The strength of comradeship in battle leads to another issue in dependency. This is the role of authority. Soldiers are obviously under authority, but they seemed in this study to have a healthy sense of dependence upon one another. Such a positive view of discipline runs counter to the general philosophy that any authority is unhealthy. Popular writings often consider an individual to be self-sufficient. We are told to be free, responsible, self-governing. This is a very optimistic notion of human nature in history. The harshness and crudity of life is left behind. An authority is considered to be an antiquated relic of the past.

Such a view fails to realize that men can enjoy freedom and self-sufficiency in a social order where there is effective authority. This would be the "rational authority" of

Fromm, freely given respect for a competent leader. One Army recruit saw this kind of leader in his lieutenant and said, "I don't mind following a man who can do everything I can do, and twice as good, but who still has patience in teaching me how to do it."

The competent leader has ability to gain the consent of those who follow him, while they keep their self-respect. This is the needed balance between dependence and independence.

Beyond the question of leaders, there is the issue of authoritative teaching. We need some guideposts, reference points, principles for living. Healthy growth requires a stable framework for individual incentive and judgment. A person needs firm reference points in order to orient himself and to regulate his interaction with others. This framework must consist both of the teaching and approval of trusted persons and the inner development of conscience and wisdom. When these reinforce each other, a person can resist giving or accepting information or attitudes that are inconsistent with his moral standards.

Without a stable framework, a person is really more dependent than he would imagine. Psychological studies show that in the absence of clear and relevant information a person is much more likely to be led by powerful figures against his own judgment. When a person has accurate information or knows where he stands on an issue, he is not nearly as likely to submit or conform to others.

Dependence is not all bad; it is a matter of balance. In the rest of this book, we will see how that balance can be maintained under different circumstances. There is the challenge of developing personal conscience in a shifting culture that requires much conformity. (Chapter 2.) Then there are temporary periods of dependency when we are very young or old, when we are sick or out of a job. How do we keep our esteem at a time when we must be sustained? (Chapter 3.) And what is to happen when we are permanently handicapped physically or chronically ill mentally? Are we still a person under these limitations? (Chapter 4.)

Most difficult of all is the question of a dependent personality. This is the individual who lives for approval, who is a chronic conformer. What form does this take and what can be done about it? (Chapter 5.) Can a person who depends on others make any investment in life himself? This is one of the ethical issues in dependency. (Chapter 6.) When we mention ethics, people are often reminded of their dependency upon God. How are we to separate out the undesirable conformity that is a part of some personalities from the religious commands of submission, surrender, and conversion? (Chapter 7.)

In all these questions there is a place for dependency. The central issue will be our acceptance of, and responsibility for, the mutual drives for autonomy and approval. There are some limitations to our self-actualization, but these must not become excuses for our failures or a way to make other people feel guilty. We have a need for affection and fellowship, but this does not mean that we bury ourselves in a crowd or pretend that we have no mind of our own. We have to move ahead in the world as it is and still find an anchor for the self.

Chapter 2

Finding an Anchor

Conformity in Urban Culture

A catchy Protestant revival tune sings, "We have an anchor that keeps the soul Steadfast and sure while the billows roll." In modern urban society, the lyrics can be extended beyond their religious meaning. Men are looking for something to anchor them in a society that has lost its old moorings. Where can a person settle down with assurance in modern society?

David Riesman concluded that the "lonely crowd" of upper-middle-class people in large American cities had settled for conformity to the opinions of others. These people have been successfully trained to pay close attention to the reaction of important people. Travelers to America report these urbanites to be more demanding of approval than Europeans, more uncertain of self and values, freer with money, friendlier, and shallower.

One European hotel clerk was bewildered by the insistence of a fur-draped guest from the United States who kept saying, "I want a better room." He pointed out the view, the quiet location, the ample space. "But," said the middle-aged woman, "it's only $25 a day!" The clerk gestured in despair and replied, "That is our most expensive rate." "Oh," said the woman, "then it *is* your best room."

She was content. So long as she *paid* the most, she thought she had the best.

This is the "other-directed" individual. He is the product of conspicuous consumption and overproduction. He need not concern himself with sustenance in the material environment. All that counts is his ability to look good before other people. He must have "influence." The problem is probably most acute with the "technological elite," the rising group of professional and managerial people whose status is based upon education. Many of these persons move from lower-middle to upper-middle class in a few years. How are they to act in this new society?

Technology has also fostered other-directedness by decreasing the death rate. In upper-middle-class society, the rate of births and deaths is low. Life expectancy is increased. People have time and means to accumulate much and to enjoy it with others.

Riesman contrasts this type of culture with the previous stage of development which produced "inner-directed" types of persons. The society of the industrial revolution and the puritan ethic was characterized by increased personal mobility, a rapid accumulation of capital, and a constant insistent expansion in the production of goods and people. Society fostered a sense of inner conviction that a person could achieve destined goals with appropriate talents. In the puritan ethic, men were to find the will of God for their lives, and work was part of that goal. In the American frontier tradition, this was the "rugged individualist," of which Theodore Roosevelt was one of the most "rugged" examples. In the "great barbecue" of industrial expansion after the Civil War, the "self-made man" seemed to be the epitome of the "free enterprise system."

This was a transitional society because it moved away from established tradition toward a new culture that has shifting potentials. We are still in some of this transitional period, and it is difficult to know where the anchor points are.

What can a person depend on today? In this time of rapid social change, two extremes are defended.

One extreme is to emphasize the private man against demands from the culture. This is the cultural heritage of Sigmund Freud. Philip Rieff, of the University of Pennsylvania, has labeled this the "triumph of the therapeutic." Culture is considered to be the inhibitor of the ego. Religion is looked upon as a cultural neurosis. Philosophy is a mass of words which screen the individual from true self-awareness. The "psychological man" is a true believer who seeks to rescue himself from the tyranny of community.

Personal insight is the key to freedom. Through self-awareness an individual is liberated from the tyranny of his family and the authoritarianism of his society.

At the same time, self-awareness protects men against the errors of their unconscious strivings. Men accept sex and hostility as drives to be channeled for self-gratification, with reasonable respect for society. The prediction and control of these drives allows a man to successfully move with independence through the sick communities in which he lives.

Some persons "use psychology" in this way. A salesman may know that he enjoys money and power. To gain these, he will deliberately size up the weakness of a buyer and appeal to status, avarice, or family. Or a professional person may know a great deal about the power of his knowledge and revel in its use. He can see that his opponent in some technical argument is getting angry. The "insightful" professional will then become "therapeutic" and say: "I believe you are showing some hostility. What has caused this?" He now wants to "help" his opponent to have "insight."

These Freudian affirmations have great appeal to

"other-directed" persons. Here is a force for healing that will also deliver the uncertain and inadequate individual from the supposed tyranny of a hostile world.

But one problem with the therapeutic approach is its acceptance of a neurotic's view of society. Karen Horney described the neurotic view as a movement against other people, away from other people, or in submission to others. Life becomes a game of one-upmanship.

In the more balanced view of Horney or Jung, society contributes to self-knowledge and partially sustains an individual in his growth. There are many things wrong with modern society, but it does not have to be viewed with the helplessness, hopelessness, and hatred of people who need psychoanalysis.

Another solution to the problem of dependence is to use psychology in the control of the society rather than the control of the individual. This is the solution of B. F. Skinner in *Walden Two*. Man is considered to be an animal that can be conditioned to gratify his desires within the framework of the complexity of social needs. By proper psychological conditioning, the need for choice can be eliminated. This will not be as repressive a system as it sounds, since choice can be made an automatic response. Only those opportunities that lead toward happiness will be presented to the individual. Social planning will eliminate the possibility of a choice toward crime, poverty, or the exploitation of others.

The problem with this secular utopia is man. Something within him rebels at this much dependency. As city planners have tried to remake slum areas, they have found that riots have followed the bulldozer. Why? Because no one considered the choices of the poor who were being displaced. In Detroit, riots started in 1966 among people who had been moved two or three times from areas of "urban renewal." Each time their plight became more desperate as the planners built sanitary homes, sanitary apartments, for someone else. It is fortunate that the massive programs of the Office of Economic Opportunity gave the poor enough voice for planners to recognize that people want something to say about the development of their own destiny. They may not change the physical characteristics of a neighborhood as quickly as a master plan would require, but with outside cooperation, it can become a better neighborhood for *them.*

Of course some people can settle for a dependent relationship and seem to be content. But what do they do with the inner resentment that springs eternally from complete conformity to the will of others?

An answer to this question came through Eaton and Weil's study of the Hutterite communities in South Dakota and Canada.[4] The Hutterite religious sect had its origin in Germany. Members of the sect came to the western United States almost a hundred years ago. Believers share a communal ownership and control of all property. Christ and the Bible are guides for faith. The community takes responsibility for all members, even to buying clothing and giving out pocket money. No wages are paid. Each person works to the best of his ability. He eats his meals in a community dining room. If he is sick, the colony pays for his care. There is social security from life to death and the religious creed gives further guarantee of security beyond physical death.

Hutterites attend public school until their fifteenth birthday and then are assigned to an agricultural job. Marriage is at age eighteen to twenty-five. With marriage comes additional responsibility such as the management of a carpentry shop, welding shop, or farm enterprise.

Hutterites live in small and nearly self-sufficient settlements in which social relationships are informal and people know each other in large families. The colonies are governed by patriarchs. The boss, or *Wirt,* and the elected preacher are the leaders of the community. There is much emphasis upon religion, with daily church services and prayers before and after each meal.

There is always a feeling of difference between Hutterites and their neighbors. The dress for the Hutterite is very plain and there is no contamination with "modern ways."

In this unified culture, a person is shielded from stress situations. As long as he conforms to what is right, he is cared for, even if he becomes sick, old, or psychotic.

How could a person become psychotic in such a placid community? It is this severe restriction of anger and the disciplinary experience of looking into the self that produces a much higher rate of depression among Hutterites than in the United States mental hospital population as a whole. Hutterites are made to feel guilty for any striving against others or unforgiving feelings. As the feelings increase, there is a loss of self-esteem and obsessive preoccupation over sins and omissions.

It should be noted that the incidence of schizophrenia among Hutterites is very low. Schizophrenia is commonly thought of as an inability to make rational choices. The sick person is literally "double-minded." In a Hutterite society, there are few choices. Culture and religion have determined what a person is to do, and if he wants to do anything else, he will have to move out into the world.

The Hutterites are a religious equivalent of *Walden Two*. They are a relatively happy and stable people. There has been no known rape, homosexuality, or preponderance of crimes in the community. Within three decades there were only ten known illegitimate children.

But there was plenty of depression and guilt.

The Family Conscience

The Hutterite child learns esteem and guilt through his family. This is the primary teaching agency of his society and religion. It is in the family that an individual learns to be sensitive to the desires of those who are about him, to know his own desires, and to decide which choices are to be made between self and others and how he is to think about himself and others when those choices have been made.

This is a description of the development of the conscience. It is the necessary guiding force for an individual to keep a balance between isolated individualism and cultural dependence in the modern world.

The development of the conscience illustrates the inseparability of self and community. What a person comes to feel within is taught him from without: custom, example of parents, play of children, the life and words of important persons, the books we read, and so on. Along with that, there is the inner striving of personal passion, individual talent, characteristic desires.

If the child is blessed with wise and patient parents, he can combine social and individual elements into a reasonable whole. This process begins when parents have enough patience to wait for the child to have capacities within himself to meet social expectations. He is expected to go to the bathroom when he is physically able to control himself, and not before. He is expected to "be on time" when he is old enough to know what time is. He is expected to tell the truth when his mind can separate out the fantasies of make-believe from the realities of life around him.

The emphasis of a considerate parent is upon the development of a moral task at a time when the child is able to respond. There is praise and there is punishment, but it is a balance between the convenience of the parents and the growing abilities of a boy or girl. Usually at age four or five, the child is able to take praise and blame into himself. He makes the words of his parents his own. It will be some time before the youngster will know how to use praise and punishment appropriately toward himself, but at least the ingredients of morality are now within.

When a child moves from home to school, there is a change in his pattern of dependence. He now learns to trust and obey older people outside the home. He also is confronted with the necessity of cooperating with other children. It is not enough to obey teacher. There are rules for play and conduct that are worked out with friends and enemies. So at age seven or eight, the child begins to "play right," whether an adult is watching or not. He has learned that this is the way to have fun with his fellows. He is beginning to use the voice of conscience for himself.

It is at this point that patterns of dependency make a great deal of difference in the way that a conscience operates. Some children have been taught absolute obedience to any whim of a parent. The child thinks there can be no question of adult rules. Literal obedience is required. So in a play situation, the child either throws all restraints away and disrupts a game, or insists that the rules must be played as he has learned them. If he keeps quiet, he is very uncomfortable, for his "conscience bothers him." In some vague way, he is aware that his parents might be displeased because he is not playing a game the way they taught him.

This is the authoritarian conscience. It is a result of the kind of discipline that has been heavily criticized by psychiatrists such as Freud and Fromm. It is fertile soil for the "overdependent personality," which was described by psychiatrists during World War II. The child will become a man who can do nothing for himself. He must always make the decisions that his parents would have made.

There is usually a good deal of bitterness in persons who have been overdisciplined. For example, a California research study reports that college girls with a high degree of prejudice toward other groups are those who ordinarily profess great love and respect for their parents. But deeper study shows that their lives are marked by much buried hostility toward their parents. They have a narrow view toward others like the narrow view that parents had of them, and the hostility that they felt from this constriction is now passed on to others.

There is similar bitterness when our children have no restrictions, that is, when they have no affection or concern shown them by parents. Veterans who reported that their parents were lacking in affection toward them were found to be very intolerant of other groups. Some bitter wound existed in themselves, and it came out toward others.

An authoritarian conscience makes others as miserable as it makes the individual. Happily, there is another possibility, which is the development of a rational conscience. This results from family relationships in which a child is encouraged to see when parents' orders should be absolutely obeyed and when circumstances should modify them. The child is encouraged to move step by step away from complete dependence upon parents. At age ten he usually can change rules if all the children vote for the change. He will abide by rules, because he feels better this way and is showing consideration for those who play with him.

If the child has taken into himself the example of wise parents, then he can begin to live by the golden rule. He replaces constraint with cooperation and judges his behavior toward others in the light of their behavior toward him. To some extent he is able to put himself in the place of another. For example, a fourth-grader told her mother: "I could take some of my nicer dolls to Penny's house, because she did say that we would play house. But she does not have many dolls and her parents can't buy her any more, so I will just take one old one that I like."

The psychological requirement for a sound conscience

is twofold. First, the individual must have an ego strong enough to make independent decisions that are in keeping with self-respect. Secondly, he must be sensitive enough to others and flexible in his judgment so that their interests are considered and met along with his own. The person is anchored in significant values that give him strength and purpose. He has received enough love and care that he can give some in return. He does not fear that he will lose himself in helping others, nor does he bargain for favors in return for his consideration.

Stretching the Self

The goals of an interdependent self, expressed in the previous paragraph, are seldom seen in every decision of life. There are numerous compromises that people make with society in order to attain ends that seem good for self and others. The problem is to know how and when to adapt.

On the one hand, some people are so concerned for the opinion of others that their ideals wear away, piece by piece, until nothing is left but the crumbs of conscience. There is a warning in the Bible from Jesus that a man might sell his soul in exchange for the world. Most of us never have that chance. We sell our soul in pieces for that part of the world that we think we must have today.

On the other hand, our conscience must be strong enough to make some adjustments without a person feeling that he is completely compromised. George Bernard Shaw illustrated this in his remark about a clergyman who had resigned from a community committee because one decision of the committee "compromised his position." Shaw exclaimed that he would be very happy to live the noble life of this uncompromising clergyman, but he had never found a way to do that and still move the community toward desirable ends. He continually found that he was having to dirty his hands with compromises, forsake a little part of his principal plans, sit down with people that he did not like, in order to get anywhere in the world.

The person who can make no compromises may be "high-minded," or he may be "closed-minded." That is, his ego may be so weak and his defenses so strong that he cannot imagine Bernard Shaw to be an honorable man. The closed-minded person is sure that the entire world is hostile, that he must arm himself against it, and that any concession is disaster.

Milton Rokeach has sought to analyze *The Open and Closed Mind*. In the book with that title, he shows that a healthy self can be stretched to depths that a closed-minded person could not imagine. Rokeach feels that we make decisions about our relationships to others on three levels of personal interaction.

First, there is the general area of opinions about groups in our society, opinions about political parties, decisions about social customs. These beliefs are not very close to the heart of a person and shift in accordance with new information or influences. A healthy person does not make a great many confusing shifts, but he will listen to a new point of view and consider the possibility of accepting or rejecting it. If the evidence is consistent with his beliefs and with his perception of reality, then he will make a change.

A closed-minded person does not have this independence of action. He is very dependent upon absolute authorities and looks to them for decisions about all kinds of things. Such dependent people may hear a great deal more evidence than an independent person hears and still stick to the same opinion. But if a person of great importance says that this new opinion is desirable, then the dependent person makes an immediate shift.

There have been a number of psychological studies to indicate the little ways in which people shift their minds on peripheral issues. Status, relationships, understanding, and experience all make a difference in what we decide.

In the case of status, psychologists set up an everyday experiment. A well-dressed, distinguished gentleman stood with a group of pedestrians at a street corner. When traffic was clear, he crossed the street in violation of the signal. Many of the people standing on the corner followed him without hesitation. Several minutes later a psychologist dressed in old clothes to suggest a person of very low status stood on the same corner. When traffic was clear he shuffled out into the street in violation of the traffic signals. One or two persons followed him. The majority of pedestrians stayed where they were.

Group influence is also suggestive. In an experimental situation, psychologists found that a student might conform to the opinion of others in a group if they argued strongly for a majority opinion. But if the student found a single ally in the group, he was more likely to hold to the answer that he thought was correct.

Also, if the student were in a group where he had little in common with others, he might retain his own point of view against strong argument. But if he were presented with contrary arguments by persons to whom he was strongly attached, he often changed his mind.

There is also the influence of knowledge and understanding of a task. For one thing, men tend to stick with their original decision if they consider the task important and have something invested in it. If they do not consider the task to be particularly important, they may conform to the opinion of others as the line of least resistance.

Again, if a person does not understand exactly what he is doing, he can be easily manipulated to do it in a different way. But if he sees exactly what is required, and understands how it is to be performed, he is much more resistant to contrary opinions.

There are plenty of illustrations of this last point in the

average household. If the husband, who is in the building trades, is laying bricks on the patio or building a porch, he does not pay much attention to advice given by wife, children, or relatives who are in other occupations. He knows what he is doing and stays with the task.

But if his wife is sick and he has to clean the house, he may be susceptible even to the word of a child who says: "Mama doesn't want it done that way. Do it like this, Daddy."

Obviously, a person's prior experience and his success in his work will be a strong buttress against conformity.

When we move from these peripheral decisions and toward the center of personality, we find that a person is more likely to have fixed opinions. Here are our ideas about God, the world, human conduct. These are some of the anchors of the self. They are not easily moved in an independent person. One study of Professor Rokeach showed that men of one religious persuasion might marry wives of a different religious persuasion, go to church with their wives, conform to the rituals of a new religious group, and yet remain essentially unchanged in their personal outlook. Their ideas about God and their attitudes toward self-conduct remained stable, even though their conduct was modified in ways that pleased their wives and made them acceptable to a new circle of friends.

It would be difficult to label these men as either "stubborn" or "dependent." We are just describing a psychological fact of human levels of decision.

At the deepest level of personality, there are those central beliefs that a person may be only dimly aware of. Here at the third level, a person relies upon some of the self-development that was previously described in a section on the conscience. An individual is personally sure of himself, or unsure. He moves and acts as though the world is friendly or unfriendly. He does not think much about this level of decision-making, but it is most basic to all the rest that happens. If a person is inadequate in this area, then we can truly say that he is "dependent." More will be said about this difficult area in succeeding chapters.

For the present, it is enough to point out that conformity to culture is not a static, once-for-all decision with most of us. We conform in part, we compromise when necessary, we comply with requests that do not contradict our basic beliefs and attitudes. A self that can stretch in this way can keep its anchor.

Chapter 3

Learning How to Lean

One reason that we seek protection in society is the knowledge that trouble may come someday and we will need help. Disease, death, natural catastrophe, business failure, may cause the most mature and adequate person to be dependent for a time. Any of us may be thrown into a temporary situation in which we need more help than we can find in ourselves for meeting a problem.

The problem that calls for situational dependency may be disease, death, dismissal from work, tyrannical parents or supervisors. It could be anything in the environment of a healthy person that demands more than he can give.

How does an adequate person, "who has never been sick a day in his life," respond? Hopefully, he will not try to be completely independent under such trying circumstances. He will learn how to depend on resources beyond himself.

The conflict between independence and dependence can be seen in persons who have some physical illness that stops their routine productivity. When symptoms of disease become so uncomfortable that the sufferer consults a physician, he will be told that he is "a sick man." Can a person accept this? Some people do not. They may fight the diagnosis, go to another physician, or ignore professional recommendations for rest, surgery, or medicine. They fear that any kind of dependence will be a total loss of independence.

Other persons become completely dependent at the first news of illness. They look to the doctor for every decision, renounce all responsibilities at home or work, become completely passive.

Then there are a large number of persons who gradually accommodate themselves to the image of themselves as "ill." They begin to say: "I can do this"; or, "I cannot do this." They are moving toward an acceptance of personal limitations.

These limitations are institutionalized when a person enters a hospital for treatment. This is the second stage in the dependency process for physical illness. The individual has accepted himself as a person with limitations that must be treated, and now he has put himself under the care of those who can correct, modify, or arrest these limitations. If illness does not immobilize a person, he may behave in many ways as he would on an ordinary day back home. In fact, modern hospitals are beginning to keep a balance between independence and dependence by recommending that some patients be in the hospital for an hour or two during the day for treatment, but then return home. If a person has come from some distance, the hospital may have a wing that is set up like a motel. There are outlets for oxygen and intercoms in each room, but otherwise it is a hotel, with hotel rates. Why should a person have to stay in a more expensive and complex medical unit for twenty-four hours a day when others need that facility more than he?

In catastrophic or immobilizing illnesses, there is an almost complete loss of independence. A person with tubes up his nose or a cast on both legs is certainly dependent upon others for every function of life except the automatic ones of his body. In some serious cases, even the automatic functions of breathing must be assisted by oxgyen or an "iron lung."

When people are in such serious condition, their best hope is to relax and let others care for them. In an accepting frame of mind, a patient receives anesthesia easily, sleeps peacefully, and usually has a less complicated recovery.

If medical and surgical procedures are successful, the patient now enters a third stage of dependency which is called convalescence. Each day he is less and less of a "patient." That is, the hospital routine and procedures upon which he was formerly dependent are now relaxed or modified. The person is encouraged to take an interest in the outside world again. He receives visitors, reads the paper, begins to think of what he will do in the world. He makes plans, talks business, renews associations.

This process of illness is much like an hourglass. At the beginning of illness, a person consciously starts to narrow down his interests toward problems in his body. Soon he is thinking more about his heartbeat, his breathing, his bowel movements, or something else in himself than about the people and events of the world from which he is temporarily detained. This narrowing of consciousness applies to people as much as it does to events. A sick person relies more and more on a few significant people. He forgets many associates and clings to those who are closest to him.

In serious illness, it is as though a person were in a tunnel. He holds to one or two persons, thinks of essential things about himself, and nothing more. But when recovery is in sight, his vision is enlarged and his world reexpands.

All of this is a natural process that should be encouraged. A person is not to think of himself as selfish or morbid if his interests are constricted during serious illness.

Psychologically he is doing the right thing; he is calling all of his energies toward a central focus of illness where a war must be won or lost. If a person considers himself worth saving, he will willingly depend on those who can help him.

When we learn to lean on others in time of illness, we usually have some thoughts about death. In fact, some patients are afraid to sleep because of an irrational feeling that they would die. But if we realistically depend upon others during illness, we are saying in effect that the issue of life and death is largely in their hands.

Ultimately this thought drives us to recognize that all our limitations can be summed up in one word: mortality. We are mortal, not immortal. We do not live forever. There will be an end to this life. For the religious person, there is the hope of a blessed existence in the life beyond this one, but religion does not guarantee an extension of mortality as such. We all die.

Yet, dying should not be a completely dependent situation. We have the ability to decide whether or not we are going to accept death. If we do accept it, our demands upon others will be easier for them to bear. An illustration of this interdependence may be seen in the following interview of a doctor and a chaplain with a patient who had been told that he was "terminally ill."

DOCTOR: What I'm really asking is, how much preparation did you have for this blow? Did you somehow have a hunch?

PATIENT: Not at all.

DOCTOR: Not at all. You were well, you were a healthy man until when?

PATIENT: Until I went into the hospital.

DOCTOR: After you had this news you must have been thinking about how it's going to be when you die, how long you are going to live. How does a man like you deal with those questions?

PATIENT: Actually, I had had so many personal griefs in

the meantime in my own life that it didn't seem like much. That's about it.

DOCTOR: Really?

CHAPLAIN: Personal griefs?

PATIENT: A series of them over a period of time.

CHAPLAIN: Do you feel like telling about it?

PATIENT: Oh, yes, that's all right.

(The patient tells of a series of family bereavements, occurring about the same time, in which he had lost both parents, a brother, and one of his grown-up children.)

DOCTOR: Yes. What Mr. _____ is really saying is, there was so much grief that it is very hard to take more grief now.

PATIENT: That's right.

DOCTOR: How can we help you? Who can help you? Is there anybody that can help with this?

PATIENT: I think so.

DOCTOR: Has anybody helped you?

PATIENT: I've never asked anybody except you.

DOCTOR: Has anybody talked with you like we are talking now?

CHAPLAIN: Well, how about these other losses? When your child died, was there anyone then that you talked with or that your wife talked with? Was this something that was left for the two of you to hold inside? Would you ever talk to each other?

PATIENT: Not very much.

CHAPLAIN: You had to hold it inside?

DOCTOR: Is your wife as grief-stricken now as she was then? Or has she kind of recuperated from this?

PATIENT: You can never tell.

DOCTOR: Is she a person who doesn't communicate?

PATIENT: She doesn't communicate about that.

(The patient describes at this point some of the difficulties he has had in his marriage, the problems of communicating, and the different attitudes toward life and death. The doctor uses this as an opportunity for drawing out the patient's own thoughts and feelings about dying.)

DOCTOR: But he is ready to think and talk about it. Yes, he should talk about it. I said you should talk about it; you have to have somebody to talk to about it.

PATIENT: My wife stops you right in the middle of a sentence. No possibility to talk to her about any of these things.

CHAPLAIN: I gather you've got a lot of faith within yourself.

PATIENT: I've done a lot of thinking within myself of how to resolve these problems.

CHAPLAIN: But I hear you saying you have the capacity for it, but you are aware that hard work isn't going to resolve the kind of conflicts that life has created at this point. You made a distinction between thinking of life and thinking of death, remember?

DOCTOR: Do you ever think about dying?

PATIENT: Yes. What were you going to say about it?

CHAPLAIN: I just wondered what thoughts you had about life in relationship to death, and vice versa.

PATIENT: Well, we'll have to admit it, but I've never thought of the worthlessness of life under such situations.

CHAPLAIN: The worthlessness . . .?

PATIENT: That if I were to die tomorrow, things would just go on.

DOCTOR: Just like nothing happened?

PATIENT: That's the way I feel.

CHAPLAIN: What gives you the strength to make a comment that one of the exciting things about coming here was that they gave you a sense of hope; they didn't just say—well, you know, look what happened with the doctor—"Look at my father; I'm sorry; it's nice to have met you"; but they said that there are some things they can do for you and they are doing them. What hit you inside, in your own desire to live? You know, with what you said about the marriage and your wife and your feelings of worthlessness, there is something inside you that has found satisfaction and desire to go on; is this faith?

PATIENT: Well, it's a kind of blind hope more than anything else, I would say; and also my church group has sustained me a great deal. I've been active in church work for years and years and years. Well, the fact that I was able to do a few things like that, which I felt were worthwhile in the community, and work like that helped me, but every ounce of work I did along that line was considered to be worthless because of the fact that it didn't contribute to making a lot of money.

DOCTOR: But that's her concept. Your concept is still that it was worthwhile?

PATIENT: I think it's worthwhile, very worthwhile.

DOCTOR: You see, I think this is the important thing. That you still have a sense of worth. This is why I think hope is meaningful to you. You still want to live; you don't really want to die, do you? That's why you came to the hospital.

PATIENT: Right.

CHAPLAIN: Were these questions you had about relationships of religion . . .?

PATIENT: Yes, I had some. For instance, one of the things was that the average patient is only going to call a chaplain; he's not going to call the psychiatrist if he happens to feel bad.

DOCTOR: That's right.

PATIENT: All right. Then the question was asked me before, by you or someone, how do I feel about the service of the chaplains. And I would say that I was dumbfounded to find that when I requested a chaplain in the middle of the night there was no night chaplain. I mean, this is just unbelievable to me, unbelievable. Because, when does a man need a chaplain? Only at night, believe me. That's the time when you get down with those boxing gloves and have it out with yourself. That's the time when you need a chaplain. I would say mostly between, in the quiet hours between, twelve and so on. . . .

DOCTOR: The early morning hours.

PATIENT: And if you were to show a chart, it would probably have a peak at about 3 o'clock. And it should be just like that—you ring the buzzer, the nurse comes, "I'd like to have a chaplain," within five minutes the chaplain shows up and you are on the road to . . .

DOCTOR: To really communicate.

PATIENT: Yes. That's the trouble with the church itself. When does a man need a minister? He needs him about three o'clock, ordinarily.[5]

The patient is still a self even though he is very, very sick. That is, he has his opinions, even some humor, and an independent perspective about death. He has chosen to depend on the doctor and the chaplain, even to the extent of resolving some problems between himself and his wife. It certainly does seem a late date for him to start to work on marriage and family relations, but why not? He does not need to "give up" as a person. There are still some relationships and attitudes that have meaning for him.

In a subsequent conversation, the wife, doctor, chaplain, and patient were together. The wife told how she had discussed with these professional persons the importance of her husband, and said, "He was the most honest and most loyal man you could ever meet." She told him how much he meant to her, offered to take him home that day and to bring him some of his church work, "which was always so meaningful to you."

The final report of the doctor in writing this description was, "It is a challenge to share with a human being his most difficult hours—and sometimes his finest."

An Uneasy Alliance

A healthy person does not submit completely to any event in this world, including death. The only complete submission is to God, and, as the dying patient has just illustrated, dependence upon God can give a person some independence in the most crucial hours of this life.

We must learn to lean, but it must always be an uneasy alliance. We depend *in part* upon others. When time and circumstances change, then the balance between dependence and independence should be altered.

Some persons use circumstances to justify a defeated attitude toward life. They have identified so much with the failures of their own life that they do not think there is anything worthy in them.

When a person has been beaten down by life, he or she may begin a vicious cycle of calling upon others for every kind of help. The more that is done for these people, the more firmly they are convinced that they can do nothing for themselves.

A minister faced this problem when Mrs. H. came to his office. She was wearing an officer's trench coat, sandals without stockings, heavy horn-rimmed glasses. Her hair was uncombed and stood straight out. It was dyed red but was gray for an inch at the roots. She was in middle age, overweight.

Mrs. H. was in great distress. Her husband was on temporary leave in the States from an overseas job. He and Mrs. H. were staying with his aunt. When they came to the city, their clothes were stolen; she did not like the living arrangements. Her husband spent all of his time with two aunts, one of whom was very ill. He had threatened to desert or divorce her, and force her to sleep alone on a couch. The minister listened during this first interview and made a second appointment for the next day.

On the following day, Mrs. H. reappeared, her appearance unchanged.

She sat down and restated her problem in much the same way as she had the previous day. She stated that her husband had threatened to divorce her or put her away.

MINISTER: What can you do about your situation?

MRS. H.: I could visit my father in the East.

MINISTER: Why don't you?

MRS. H.: I wouldn't have enough money to return. I have to be here in time to leave. (This became her only security, as she saw it, to be here so she could get home.) Otherwise, I would be deserted.

MINISTER: If your husband is as cruel as you state, perhaps this is not too bad. Maybe you should divorce him on grounds of mental cruelty. I think you have a case.

MRS. H.: No, the marriage vows say "for better or for worse." I know some people who have been divorced, and their second marriages are usually worse than the first. Besides, I have no occupation. I don't know how to do anything but be a housewife. A cruel husband is an occupational hazard of being a housewife. (This was said quizzically, while smiling at her joke.)

She finally concluded that there was nothing she could do but stay where she was until her husband was ready to return to their home, and after much repetition of the situation she again decried her husband's lack of attention.

MRS. H.: He could at least take my clothes to the laundry when he takes his.

MINISTER: But the fact is he is not taking your clothes to the laundry. So you may have to go yourself.

MRS. H.: But this is his responsibility. He has the car.

MINISTER: But he is not assuming this responsibility, and you are only two blocks from the nearest laundry.

MRS. H.: And carry my laundry bag down the street?

MINISTER: If that is what it takes.

MRS. H.: That is what I thought I had a husband for, to be responsible for me.

MINISTER: But he is not being responsible, so you will have to be responsible for yourself. You are an adult. You will have to act like one. There is really no excuse for going without clean clothes and looking as you do with laundries as available as they are.

MRS. H.: The Bible says that you have to be like a child to enter the Kingdom of Heaven. It also says "consider the lilies, they spin not. . . ."

MINISTER: The Bible does not say we should be childish. The reference to the lilies refers to worry about the future. It suggests that we be responsible for each day as it comes. There is at least one thing in this whole situation you can be responsible about. That is your looks. It is not necessary to look so disheveled.

MRS. H.: I look the way I feel.

MINISTER: If you start looking better, then you will begin feeling better. If you don't start taking a little responsibility for yourself, your husband might have every reason to leave you.

MRS. H.: There is nothing I can do. I have to save my money. I don't have a car; I don't have any clothes; I don't have a washing machine. You are like the Levite in the Good

Samaritan. I have been robbed and beaten and you have passed me by. A Good Samaritan would bind my wounds and clothe me.

MINISTER: I'm trying to give you some mental clothing, and you won't accept it. If you don't, you will find yourself in a mental hospital, because that is where you look as if you belong. You don't have to spend all your money to look better. You can go to the nearest Salvation Army store and buy some used clothing that would be suitable and clean.

The conversation continued to revert back to her husband and what he didn't do. She began to weep and wept violently for two or three minutes. I watched, saying nothing. Her tears stopped as suddenly as they began. After more conversation she stated that she was often on the verge of weeping and that her husband threatened to put her in an institution because of her tears.

I told her that her tears were not very impressive, suggesting that a change in behavior and action would do more to help her situation. After some discussion, I gave her a coat from a missionary box as a beginning of her change, insisting that she continue by going to the laundry and then buying some other clothes. Again she referred to the impossibility of doing so because of her lack of a car and a washing machine. If she were only home, then she would manage. I reminded her that she was not at home, that she was in the city, and that laundries and buses were available. Further, I suggested that, if she were interested in washing her clothes, none of these were really essential. I told her of some French women I had seen laundering their clothes in the river without soap. I implied that she was without excuse.

MRS. H.: I know what you are trying to do to me. I remember a movie in which a Negro and a white man were Army buddies. The Negro had an artificial leg because of a wound, and he was afraid to walk. He was afraid to try. His friend was trying to talk him into it. Finally he called him a yellowbellied nigger. This made the Negro so angry that he lunged out of his wheelchair because of his anger. That's what you're trying to do to me. You're trying to make me so angry that I'll do something. You're trying to tell me that I don't have to have all the conveniences of my home to do

something. I remember a situation in the Bible where somebody didn't have what they needed. . . .

MINISTER: Samson had nothing but the jawbone of an ass,
but he slew thousands.

MRS. H.: You mean I'm supposed to take up my jawbone,
whatever it is, and do something with it?

MINISTER: I think that is what you had better be doing if
you want to regain your mental health. The first step is to
comb your hair and begin looking like a woman again.

MRS. H.: My husband doesn't make me feel like a woman.

MINISTER: You are a woman. You will have to do what you
can for yourself regardless of how he makes you feel.

There was further discussion of her husband's attitudes,
actions, and threats. I commented that if he were really that
obnoxious, I would just tell him to go to hell and forget about
it.

MRS. H.: I really couldn't do that. It's always this way
when we come back. Perhaps I have it coming. I rule things
pretty much my own way at home, and it's not too easy for
him.

MINISTER: Now he has the upper hand, and he is getting
even.

MRS. H.: That is probably so.

MINISTER: Then, in that case, you had better just face the
music; but you can help yourself and make it a little easier to
keep your sanity by doing some of the things I have suggested.

On this note the interview came to an end. This was Friday.
I suggested that she return on Tuesday. She came in for the
third interview on Monday.

THE THIRD INTERVIEW

Mrs. H. was something of a transformed woman in appearance. She had her hair in curlers, and it looked very much
neater than it had on her previous visits. She had rouge on her
face, her glasses were clean, and she had on the coat I had
given her as well as a different dress that looked very well on
her. She wore white socks and a pair of moccasin-type slippers.
All in all, she looked like an average housewife on an average

morning on an average street rather than an escapee from a mental hospital. She wanted to know how she looked.

MINISTER: Well, you look much better.

MRS. H.: Well, I don't feel much better.

She began to explain the events of the weekend. Apparently the crisis had passed when the aunt who had been in the rest home died. The husband and the other aunt were preparing for the funeral, which was to take place the next day. It was also apparent that the husband had spent all his money. She thought that the money in her possession was all that they had to last for the next fifty days of their vacation, though they might draw some on the bank in Alaska. He was being paid while on leave. She was very disgusted with this turn of events and said that that was the way his relatives always treated him. They simply used him for all he was worth. He really thought he was going to get some money out of the estate of the aunt who had died, but she doubted that he would. In discussing these things over the weekend, he had even said "dear" to her twice.

MINISTER: Well, the natural course of events is returning your husband to you.

MRS. H.: I think that's right.

MINISTER: It sounds to me as if your husband has acted like a man who's been on shore leave.

MRS. H.: Yes, that's the way it was.

MINISTER: He's the sort of man who has to have a very secure situation. All his work has been in very structured jobs in which he knew exactly what every day would bring. When he is loose and on his own, he doesn't know how to behave and act.

MRS. H.: Yes, that is right. I married for security. It doesn't look like it turned out that way. I guess I'm just going to have to live with it.

There was a little further friendly exchange, and then the telephone rang and a man came to the door. Our conversation was interrupted. When I returned to her, she said, "Well, you must be awfully busy as a minister in the city." And I said, "Well, yes, there are usually enough things going on to keep my hands full and my time occupied." She replied that she would not take any more of my time that morning. She thought things would work out. She left, thanking me for my time.[6]

The minister is uneasy about the defeated attitude of Mrs. H. and he helps her to be uneasy about her dependency. It is true that life has been hard on her and that she has suffered some real misfortune, but it will be worse if she continues to think of herself as a helpless individual.

The Work of Worrying

Some people defend themselves against hope by saying: "But I cannot decide what to do. I am just worried sick by all that has happened." The alliance of these people with trouble is firm and fast.

But such people have misused "worrying." This can be a very constructive lever in moving away from an alliance with adverse circumstances. Of course, this is only possible in more or less healthy people who are not preyed upon by chronic fears and ill-defined anxieties. I am not writing now for the neurotic who is consumed by "free-floating anxiety" that will attach itself to any circumstance. I am writing now about the healthy person who is warned by some communication, some threat in his environment, some physical symptom, that he is in danger.

How does a person worry constructively in the face of trouble? First, by himself or with others, he makes the discrimination that I have just pointed out in the previous paragraph. He comes to see that there is some objective reason for him to be filled with fear or to feel weak. It is not just something "in his mind." If it were, he would probably have a history of vague feelings of discomfort, states of panic, and general anxiety over a period of years.

A person feels better about himself if he can say: "Something has happened *to me*," rather than "There is something wrong *with* me." I do not wish to suggest that a person should isolate the illness or catastrophe from him. It is now in him or upon him, and he must live with it. He must also take some responsibility for the circumstances under which this difficulty appeared. All that I am saying is that some specific circumstances did have a tremendous effect upon the way he is living now. It is an observable threat that comes from causes that are considered external to the self.

An example of this discrimination can be seen in the thoughts of some patients about cancer. On the one hand, there are people who recognize that they "have" a malignancy and that it must be treated. On the other hand, there are people who look upon the disease as an extension of themselves, as a consequence of their own evil lives. When I have asked these people what is so evil about them, they usually have no definite answer. All they can say is that they must have done something very bad to have such a dread disease. Their worrying would certainly be unprofitable, because it is based on a vicious view of the self.

In contrast, there is a second statement that can be made about constructive worrying. The person who has distinguished a disease or disaster from himself can, with the help of others, begin to understand just how dangerous the alien force is. For example, before an operation a patient may discuss with his surgeon the meaning of his symptoms and the probable outcome of his operation. He will be aware of what a disease can do to him if it remains unchecked, and he can be told what pains or bodily changes to look for as danger signs after the operation. Then he can be reassured that medication will be available to help him when a change of his condition indicates danger.

From the example of many surgical cases, Dr. Irving Janis has concluded that the "work of worrying" is as important for successful surgery as "the work of mourning" is for the resolution of grief.[7] If a person knows what he is facing and prepares himself for it, then he undergoes discomfort as a natural consequence of his decision to allow the operation. He has worried through the problem to a successful resolution.

If a person has "refused to worry," he may have a most uncomfortable convalescence. For one thing, if the patient suffers physical discomfort that he did not anticipate, he may be angry with the surgeon and the hospital. He may alternate between unrealistic feelings of complete helplessness toward a magical, godlike doctor, and irrational fears and projection of blame upon personnel. He is a difficult patient because he did not consider realistically the pain and discomfort of a surgical procedure. He needed the work of worrying.

Thirdly, the work of worry will arm a person against dangerous attacks. He does not place himself in circumstances where he is vulnerable, if he can help it. Or if he does find that he is overcome by more pain, debt, or grief than he can stand, he calls for help from friends or professional persons. The threat may be entirely psychological, as when a young person is consistently ignored by a parent, when a wife is always sneered at by her husband, or when a man is blamed for every mistake by his boss.

Whatever the source of threat may be, the individual seeks to "worry" enough to stay out of trouble when he can and use whatever defensive measures are possible when he is in a jam. He is trying to be as independent as possible in a very compromising situation.

For example, a university president was worried because friends told him that a financier on his board was "out to get him." The president had seen a conflict of interest, for the financier was chairman of a finance committee of the university and most of the investment funds of the university were in his bank. The financier was furious when the president requested that future investment funds should be deposited impartially in a number of banks.

At a subsequent board meeting, the financier accused the president of misappropriating funds for his own personal use. The financier, who was greatly respected in the state, was listened to without question by most board members. The president was immediately suspended without a hearing.

The president was in turmoil. He was torn between panic, anger, and despair. He sought the counsel of a close friend who recommended that a complete audit of all university finances should be made. The president had "worried" enough about the financier that he had kept all his expense records for some time. When the auditors came to his expenses, they found the discrepancy which was at the root of the financier's accusation. The president had charged an airline ticket to the university for a lecture trip on which he received an honorarium.

But the accountants also found that the president had a record of two contacts with prospective donors along the way to the lectureship, and that he had the canceled personal check that he had sent to the university treasurer for the plane fare between his last contact and the place of his lectureship. The auditors issued a report that all financial affairs of the university, including those of the president, were in good order.

Several months later the president resigned and took an attractive position with an established foundation. In retrospect he saw that he had "worried" enough to save his reputation. But he had not been apprehensive enough about the entrenched interest represented in the university when he accepted a position there. If he had really "worried" realistically, he would either have rejected the invitation to the university, or requested that certain reforms be made by the trustees before he accepted the position of president.

But who would really know what he was up against until there was some testing in the situation? If we move with faith and hope, we usually assume that some difficult problems can be cleared up. We take normal precautions, but usually do not foresee how fast some trouble can spread. It probably will not help for us to reproach ourselves with hindsight. The advice of Jesus is better: "Do not take thought for tomorrow, for tomorrow will take thought for the things of itself. Sufficient to the day is the evil thereof." We can worry as far as we can see, and then we might as well stop.

Chapter 4

Protection for Life

The example of the university president was from the life of an experienced and mature man. It is certainly not presented as the model for everyone who wants to become independent. For one thing, he is a man, and as we will try to show in this chapter, men have some advantages over women in the struggle for independence. Also, the man obviously has many talents. His condition is quite different from the person who has only one talent, or who has been handicapped by brain damage or mental deficiency. We require much, much less in the way of independence from such persons.

There is also the factor of age. There certainly was a time when the university president was very dependent, that time being childhood. And it will come again to him in the later years of retirement. All these differences from the mature man should be noted.

But age, sex, physical and mental deficiencies should not be lumped together. There are some obvious differences between these types of dependency. Childhood is a time when we lean upon other people, but this is a *growth* dependency. We express such powers as we have at the age of two, five, or ten and hope for the day when we will be more adequate and able to do for others as they have done for us.

Physical and mental handicaps are part of *deficiency* dependency. The individual must always cope with some handicap. He may obtain some independence, but it will be kept within specific limits that do not apply to other people.

With these distinctions in mind, there still is a central question in growth and deficiency motivation: Can we be a person without expressing the full range of normal self-actualization? Are we only half a person when we have some handicap, or when we are very young or very old?

Affection and Autonomy

These questions begin with birth. Who could be more dependent than an infant? Yet this is a little individual. Relatives soon remark about the characteristic ways in which a baby responds. He is not a blank tablet on which parents may write their own prescriptions for a new life.

Of course the child of one or two years of age must find the gratification of many motives in mother and father. A healthy baby shows anxiety when mother leaves temporarily. For she is his preferred source of support. During World War II, a substantial proportion of English children under two years of age did not make satisfactory progress in a day nursery. They lost weight at a time in life when other children, at home with their parents, were gaining weight. Yet the children in the day nursery received double the rations available to children in homes.

Obviously, the presence of a mother is very important to the infant, but it is the *kind* of presence that makes all the difference in the development of a dependent or independent individual. As the section on the development of conscience has shown, a parent can overcontrol the child and restrict his autonomy. Or the parent may allow the child to explore his world within limits of safety. This latter way calls for a combination of acceptance and judgment. On the one hand, a parent loves the child as a person rather than as an extension of the parent, and delights in signs of personality and character in the infant. On the other hand, the parent protects the child from too much strain or stress.

As the child grows into the preschool stage, an independently-minded parent will expect some initiative on the part of the child. He should be able to dress himself, attend to himself in the bathroom, solve minor problems, and play alone without constant attention. In fact, healthy parents usually show some impatience with children who behave in a very dependent manner at age five. This is not always too helpful to the child, who is in conflict between his trend toward initiative and his previous patterns of dependence. The problem for the parent is to accept some of the dependence and to reward the independence.

What is it that the parent rewards? If it is conformity to the parents' opinions and convenience for one adult member of the family, then the child may become quite restricted in his expressions. But if curiosity, originality, fancifulness, and constructiveness are encouraged, the child will be more aggressive, friendly, and independent.

A parent cannot develop a socially acceptable independence in a child without much expenditure of patience and time. The three-year-old must be taught how to control the TV so that he can watch his favorite program. The five-year-old must have many lessons on tying shoes or choosing the skirt that goes with a blouse. The seven-year-old must be taught a routine of getting ready for school without too many reminders. Throughout these many processes, a parent shares his knowledge with a child, makes corrections, and above all, offers encouragement. He imparts to the child a feeling that a reasonable task can be accomplished if the child receives instruction and resources. Out of this training comes achievement. The child comes to believe that he can accomplish most of the tasks assigned to him by society if he receives reasonably clear instructions and is given the resources necessary for their accomplishment.

This becomes a spontaneous part of the personality. I once saw an eleven-year-old boy draw engine diagrams on a home blackboard. He proudly annouced to me that he had just found the place for venting gases from each stroke of the engine. Ten years later, the same young man was building a new machine with aluminum. In describing its operation, he said, "Of course, Daddy helped me to figure out the stress patterns."

It was all very natural. The parents had not "pushed" any of their children, but they had shown real affection for their initiative, had tried to encourage their interests in creative ways, and had the intelligence and training to provide answers for technical questions.

I stress the natural and spontaneous elements in achievement because there is a tendency in middle-class American society to drive children toward achievement. Little consideration is given to the interests and talents of the youngster; he is considered to be little more than an extension of the parents' striving toward new social heights. An example of the pervasiveness of this pushing was seen by one parent when a high school counselor saw him at a P.T.A. meeting. The counselor said: "I had a long talk with your son yesterday. He had made C in solid geometry. He will never get a national honors scholarship that way. I doubt that he would even get a science fellowship without all A's and B's in mathematical subjects. I told him that he surely would not want to let his father down."

The parent knew what the counselor meant. Great status came to parents in that community when their children received scholarships, especially those in science. So he thanked the counselor but added a word of caution: "Have you asked my son if he is interested in mathematics? It is my impression that he leans more toward the humanities. As a matter of fact, I am not too concerned about any honors that he would win. We have never discussed it."

Parents can help children to be more independent. But they are not the only influences upon a growing youngster. Psychologists have found that grade school children are influenced toward certain behavior more by other children than they are by adults. In adolescence, the influence of other adolescents will be very dominant. The young person is concerned about how well he is accepted by people of his own sex, and increasingly by the opposite sex. He or she wants to be in with the right crowd, say things that make sense and are clever, be respected, and still have a good time.

The adolescent is often uncertain and confused about the way to be independent in his crowd and his confusion is often shared by parents as well. The parent, like the child, is caught between the need for protection and initiative. He wants the young person to be on his own, yet fears that he will wreck the car, be seduced, or run with the wrong crowd.

If the parent is absorbed in conformity to his culture, he will not be very helpful to his children in their struggle toward autonomy. For one thing, he will read their actions in the light of his insecure status. A high school principal may expect his daughter to "be smarter" or "apply herself" more than other children. A businessman may be furious about a son's car accidents because he thinks people will laugh at him at his insurance agency.

Neither of these men will be able to see any problem of the adolescent in context. It will all be redrawn in the light of adult insecurities, or perhaps in the light of adult fantasies concerning what fun it would be if the man could be a boy again.

A more realistic parent might discuss with an adolescent the difficulties of one generation's understanding of another. An adult can share the experiences that he had at a younger age and tell what he learned from them. This is a giving of himself. In return, an adolescent can be challenged to tell what is happening in his generation. If he wants his parents to "understand him," then he will have to share some of himself with them. The mutual understanding will probably not be complete, but it can often come close enough for a parent to trust a child despite parental anxieties, and for the growing youngster to feel that his parents wish the best for him and are setting reasonable restrictions on activities.

Most of all, the adolescent needs to learn something about attitudes. The way in which parents deal with him, and the way they talk about his friends and their friends, will be the most constructive or destructive part of the parent-child relationship. An accurate assessment of others is a part of the wisdom that a parent can pass on to a younger person. Conformity to the parent's opinion is not greatly prized.

When parents hear this generalized type of advice, some of them will say: "But I just do not know what to tell my child"; or, "I tried to find out what other parents are allowing for their child, and allow the same for mine." To some extent, these parents are saying that they are not so sure of themselves that they can make independent decisions about an adolescent's behavior. They must depend in part upon the opinions of others. There is an element of cultural dependence in our decisions about conduct, and I have not tried to minimize this. But I am warning against an unthinking conformity to society that will comfort the parents or add to their social status.

Parents may also observe that some youngsters do not want to make any decisions on their own. They do not care to move out of a childhood state of dependency. When this occurs in an adolescent, we call him immature. When it continues into young adulthood, we may refer to it as "maternal overprotection."

The Weaker Sex

We judge people mature or immature, dependent or independent, according to their age and abilities. We also make these judgments on the basis of sex, or more properly, gender. Masculinity is associated with more aggressive, hostile, and assertive behavior than femininity. Femininity usually calls to mind a feeling of receptivity, a nurturing, accepting, sustaining set of attitudes.

These cultural expectations, which may be rooted in biological differences, create different problems for boys and girls. Society encourages the adolescent boy to become independent. If he was previously overly dependent, parents and peers push him toward a different kind of behavior. This forces the boy to inhibit overt dependent behavior, and this inhibition may continue into adulthood.

Dependent behavior is socially more acceptable for girls. And a girl who is excessively dependent as an adolescent is more likely to remain dependent through the early adult years. Such women will consult their mothers before making major purchases, prefer to live close to their families, and feel a close tie to relatives. In contrast, girls who show self-sufficiency during adolescence have affection for their homes but are quite happy in their emancipation from parents.

A man is tempted to act as though he had no dependent needs. The woman is tempted to submerge her personality in a dependent role as wife, mother, or mousy stenographer.

Mrs. Valerie Goldstein has declared that the major problem of a woman is the negation of her selfhood.[8] Both biology and culture would allow a woman to be a very dependent being. A girl attains womanhood quite naturally —merely by the maturation of her body. A boy is required by society to prove himself, to *do things* that will make him a man. His sister has only to wait for biological processes to mature. This waiting is perpetuated by society into adulthood, when the girl makes herself available for a date or marriage. Her purpose is to be a desirable love object. The man's purpose is to be active and self-assured in proposals.

When married, the woman can again be quite passive, both physically and psychologically, and still become a mother. The man is required to be active, both in sexuality and in the work he does to provide funds to care for his enlarged family. When a child is born, the mother is his closest associate in the first few years of life. She can withdraw into "motherhood" and leave all decisions outside that charmed circle to her husband.

How can this dependency pattern be modified? Theologically and philosophically, women can be challenged with the assurance that they were created to be persons, no matter what role they may fulfill in family or society. From this follows a psychological teaching, that the best wife and mother role is fulfilled by an adequate individual. A "clinging vine" is not a very stimulating companion. This is first known by the husband, and it is later known by the children. As they grow up, they ask, "What did you do as a child, Mommy?" and delight to know all the details. They want to identify with an individual, with someone who has been an active, living person.

In adolescence, there is much talk about the characteristics of parents, and the young people are most comfortable in relationship to parents who have well-defined qualities that are acceptable. So, for example, a group of teen-age girls were decorating the patio of a country estate before a summer party for underprivileged children. One girl said to another: "Hey, your mother has been out here running the lawn mower for an hour. How come?" Her companion grinned and replied: "Oh, I don't know, my mother does lots of funny things like that. She just likes to work in the yard, so I asked her to come along and help here. She does a pretty good job, don't you think?"

Besides philosophy and theology, women should consider a biological problem. If they tie their self-development to the natural processes of life, then they will be "unproductive" in the last third of their existence. The menopause is the highest time of depression among women, and they may be depressed because of their feelings about a biological change more than because of the change itself. A woman may say to herself: "I'm not really important without my children, or the possibility of having children." With the menopause, and with the movement of children out of the household by the time a woman is forty-five, her hiding places are disappearing. But if marriage and parenthood have been opportunities for self-development and fulfillment, she can survive the adjustments of this change in life situation. She is a person, no matter how she is related to those who contribute to her personal growth.

Limiting Factors in Life

The dependency of age and sex has a biological root, but it is in the direction of growth and fulfillment. The protective environment of the family or culture is gradually relaxed as the child grows older, or the girl becomes an autonomous individual.

But there are other biological limitations that do not allow so much growth. There may be brain damage from birth, mental retardation, or crippling illness that drastically alter the potentials of an individual. Under such limitations, how can a person be anything but dependent?

A common misconception is to answer this question by negating personality. That is, the handicapped individual is treated as though he were different from normal people in almost every respect. He is not considered to have the feelings or desires that others have. He is different, sick or something like that. At least he is not "our kind of person."

In reality, we are all limited in some ways, but these limitations are more conspicuous or circumscribing in some of us than in others. Physical defects do make a difference, but they do not make different people.

In the case of children with brain damage, there certainly are some definite limitations in the way that they perceive and respond, but their feelings and attitudes are as sensitive—if not more sensitive—than those of other children.

This was illustrated in one community as a group of six-year-olds were driven to kindergarten each day by a mother who took her son along. He was the same age as the other children, but had suffered some brain injury that prevented him from speaking whole sentences, or even part of a sentence in a comfortable way. But he could recognize words, and had learned to read traffic signs before the other children in the car pool.

Although there was no special school for him to attend in the community, he felt much acceptance through his half hour with the other children each morning and afternoon. One of the favorite games of the group was to point to a sign on the road and ask the handicapped boy to say what it was. He would pronounce "stop," and smile as the children congratulated him for learning to read so well.

One of the children in the car pool summed up the thesis of this chapter when she told her father: "Charlie is just like us, except that he can't talk so well. He reads road signs better than any of us, and enjoys it."

Persons who are mentally retarded present another opportunity for people to see how much they are like each other. It is true that some people are so severely handicapped that they must be institutionalized, but about 90 percent of mentally retarded persons are capable of functioning to some extent in a normal environment.

There is a need, of course, to draw some distinctions between the dependent and independent needs of persons
with these limitations and those who do not have such
severe restrictions.

For one thing, we do need to accept the seriousness of a
retardate's limitations. He cannot perceive and respond as
fast as other people, and should not be placed in positions
where this is required. For example, the quick choices that
many of us make in normal society may confuse a retarded
person and cause him to become anxious, withdrawn, or
angry. He is more comfortable with an established routine
in which he knows what or who is coming next and how
he is expected to react.

At the same time, a retarded person should be allowed
to express and clarify his feelings and gain self-confidence
through some experiences of success. After being introduced to several routine chores at home, or various tasks
in a sheltered workshop, he can be asked which he likes
the best. When he has had time to make a decision, he
should be encouraged to continue with those that are most
satisfying to him and praised for his completion of them.
His work may not be as fast as others, but it may be thor-
ough. He is a "success" within the limits of our expectations.

A third suggestion is that we notice the way in which
retarded persons do grow. Even though they lack some
mental capabilities, they are aware of their own bodily
changes and know something of the age group with which
they would normally belong. So, educable adolescents are
most comfortable in a school for the retarded with other
persons of their own size and interests. In a community
facility, such as a Sunday school for the retarded, they are
pleased with literature that shows adolescent boys and
girls in activities appropriate in our culture for that age.
The words in the lesson may be simplified to a first- or
fifth-grade level, but the stories are about boys and girls of

age fifteen or sixteen—just like the adolescents who are in this class.

A fourth suggestion is that society be used to support rather than repress a retarded person. This is a difficult achievement in a success-oriented culture where people are expected to be completely adequate, and yet are called upon to conform to cultural norms. If we were in the Hutterite society which was described in a previous chapter, it would be easier to find a supported place for a person with limited capabilities.

In a competitive culture, a dependent person can obtain some independence through organizations like "sheltered workshops." A retarded person who can be educated to perform productive tasks would be in a shop where instructions and timetables were geared to a retarded person's level of learning and performance. He works for wages and has confidence that his product is worth something. In time, he may leave a sheltered workshop for a specified position in society where the limitations are seldom noticed and he is able to think of himself as being more like other people than different from them. There is still an element of dependence in the individual, but it is not complete. He can be seen and respected as a person.

There are other examples that could be given of people with chronic illness, defects that severely limit movement. In such cases, a person cannot find fulfillment through work. He may be completely dependent physically upon others. Some of the problems that are raised by this condition will be discussed in Chapter 6 on the ethics of dependency.

Chapter 5

The Mask of Approval

Anything on Approval

In the musical *Porgy and Bess* white police officers question the residents of Catfish Row about a murder. They learn nothing. Finally, one of the officers asks if each person will swear that he saw nothing on the night of the murder. Immediately all hands are raised and a chorus sweetly chimes, "We swears, Boss."

The black man of the 1920's had learned what the white man wanted him to say and he said it. The black man's feelings, observations, and objections were never revealed. The minority protected itself from the majority by wearing the mask of approval. The man of color swore to anything that the white man desired, or at least it seemed that way when white officers were looking for evidence.

The mask of approval was dropped when the white men left. The residents of Catfish Row could be themselves again.

But what happens when a person cannot drop his mask? What if a person has begun to learn as a youth that he must hide himself from everyone in order to be protected? It is not just black against white, it is one vulnerable self against a whole world that would crush him, or so it seems to the inadequate person.

The mask may seem to be stuck to the person, so much so that he does not even know his own desires. He is conforming, cautious, persuasible. Other people may see a task as dull and boring, but a conforming individual may say it is very desirable because some important person has asked him to do it.

Many pleasant sounds come out of the mask. It is popular talk, small talk, words and phrases that should sound good to those who have power. Sounds may come forth for hours at a time and still no one will know what manner of person was speaking.

We do know that the sound can be changed. If a person of importance changes the subject, or contradicts the directions of the sounds, they will change. Soon we realize that we have faced Talkative, the son of Say-well, of Prating Row. So John Bunyan described in *The Pilgrim's Progress* a man who could discuss any topic with Christian:

TALK.: What you will. I will talk of things heavenly, or things earthly; things moral, or things evangelical; things sacred, or things profane; things past, or things to come; things foreign, or things at home; things more essential, or things circumstantial; provided that all be done to our profit.[9]

Mr. Talkative would say nothing about himself, because he was unknown. He had conformed so well that he had no real knowledge of his personal desires. He had learned that submission to others would entail the fewest risks of social rejection and threat to self-esteem. He was always trying to ward off anticipated failures.

Unfortunately, the attempts are self-defeating. The person who has given all on approval has little ability to recognize what is going on within him. Anger and resentment build up in the depths of his soul. He does not like to do as others tell him and always smile and be happy, but he cannot accept these frightful thoughts within him. Yet it keeps on showing in little ways. The smile is forced, the conversation is strained. The conformist seems anxious to leave, and yet he stays on. It is a miserable kind of double-mindedness.

Despair is warded off by being a "proper" person. The approval-motivated individual says the right thing about himself, holds all of the right attitudes, reflects all the virtues he can find of an adjusted individual.

But rewards are so few for trying too hard in this way! So the sublimated hostility and self-contempt remain. Everything has been given on approval, and so little has come in return.

Conformity and Character

When the mask of approval has shaped the self, then we have a dependent person. This is not the healthy ego who has adapted himself to temporary threat, a normal person who has complied with social requirements. This is not the physically handicapped person whose reason for dependence is objectively demonstrated. We are talking now about people who are generally submissive, low in self-confidence, full of conventional values, filled with inner need to conform.

When experiments have involved group pressure with a large number of experimental subjects, leaders can be differentiated from the most compliant followers. There are definite personality characteristics of those who make independent decisions and those who depend upon the decisions of others.

In addition to the observation of others, there are specific statements that independent and dependent persons choose for themselves. Here are some illustrative items that are marked "true" by the independent subjects.

Sometimes I rather enjoy going against the rules and doing things I'm not supposed to.

I like to fool around with new ideas, even if they turn out later to be a total waste of time.

A person needs to "show off" a little now and then.

At times I have been so entertained by the cleverness of a crook that I have hoped he would get by with it.

It is unusual for me to express strong approval or disapproval of actions of others.

I am often so annoyed when someone tries to get ahead of me in a line of people that I speak to him about it.

Compared to your own self-respect, the respect of others means very little.

In contrast, dependent persons choose items such as these:

I am in favor of very strict enforcement of all laws, no matter what the consequences.

It is all right to get around the law if you don't actually break it.

Most people are honest chiefly through fear of being caught.

These extreme conformists show an inconsistent moralistic attitude toward life. In addition, they show a great desire for clarity and certainty about all decisions. They dislike any kind of ambiguity, so they choose statements such as these:

I don't like to work on a problem unless there is a possibility of coming out with a clear-cut and unambiguous answer.

Once I have made up my mind, I seldom change it.

Perfect balance is the essence of all good composition.

There is also much preference for conventional values as in the following:

I always follow the rule: business before pleasure.

The trouble with many people is that they don't take things seriously enough.

I am very careful about my manner of dress.

Despite all this caution, anxiety remains. The conforming persons often check items such as these:

I am afraid when I look down from a high place.

I am often bothered by useless thoughts that keep running through my head.

I often think, I wish I were a child again.

I often feel as though I have done something wrong or wicked.

The reason for the anxiety is a feeling of distrust toward other people. A cluster of these statements were checked by conformists:

When I meet a stranger, I often think that he is better than I am.

Sometimes I am sure that other people can tell what I am thinking.

I wish that I could get over worrying about things I have said that may have injured other people's feelings.

I commonly wonder what hidden reason another person may have for doing something nice for me.

People pretend to care more about one another than they really do.[10]

When people are this distrustful of others, we really cannot say that they are of good character. Despite all their attempts to be proper, something is missing. There is a deviousness about their ways with men that causes them to be ignored, exploited, or rejected by others.

Sometimes the dependent person is painfully aware that all is not well. How does he cope with the discrepancy between what he sees in others and what he sees in himself? One typical reaction is to blame himself, to doubt his own accuracy of judgment, to say that he does not read or understand things well. This is consistent with the self-contempt that keeps him dependent.

Or he may blame other people, express doubt about their ability to see things whole. Others may be thought of as deceitful and misleading. This would justify the deep distrust that the dependent person has of those about him.

The loss of character comes out when the dependent

persons are asked to describe their feelings about a situation, to make an independent judgment on a problem. Quite often, a conformist will be evasive and shallow. If he is asked to describe an experience, he may say, "Exactly what do you mean by experiences?" Or if people want to know how he felt when listening to a certain person, he may say, "Oh, I didn't feel anything, I felt normal." If an associate notices that the conformist votes "yes" at one time and "no" when the same question comes up in a different group, the conformist will protect himself by saying, "Oh, well, people perceive things differently and how are we to know who is right?"

When confronted with actual errors, a conformist reverts either to self-blame or projection of blame. It is most difficult for him to admit forthrightly that he was wrong.

The self-protective evasiveness of a dependent person is a constant source of annoyance to those who want frank and realistic answers. The resulting dilemma is like Br'er Rabbit and Tar Baby. When Br'er Rabbit, skipping down the bunny trail, finds that Tar Baby does not respond to his "hi y'all," he cannot restrain his impatience. First one fist and then the other smashes into Tar Baby. Tar Baby will not let go. Soon hands and feet are stuck in a compliant mass.

Now the dependent person has his impatient tormentor just where he wants him. At every point he has said "yes" and glued his approval to every opinion. The person who makes demands of the dependent individual will soon find himself frustrated by one yes after another.

Here is part of a tar-baby drama. A professor has been approached by a student who "wants help."

STUDENT: Sir, I just feel that I am not doing my work as well as I should.

PROFESSOR: Well, let's see what your grades are. Oh, yes, you made 82 on the last test. You seem to be doing very well, very well indeed.

STUDENT: Yes, sir, thank you sir. But I'm not satisfied. I should be doing so much better. I know that I am capable of much better work.

PROFESSOR: Perhaps so. Well, you might try a little harder (*starts to rise*). There will be another test in a week.

STUDENT (*still seated*): Yes, sir. It's those tests that bother me. I seem to have missed some of the emphases that you have made. Lots of other people seem to have the same trouble. We find the tests confusing.

PROFESSOR: Huh? Well, I think that if a man studied, he should not have trouble with my tests. Why don't you spend more time studying?

STUDENT: Oh, I study sir, and I did not mean to criticize the test. I guess it is just something in me, I don't see what I ought to see in your questions. Maybe it is just something wrong with me. Of course, I have always made A's before, so I just do not know what it could be.

PROFESSOR (*with growing irritation*): Well, I don't know either. Why don't you talk to my student assistant about this? He makes out all the grades.

STUDENT: Yes, sir. I have talked to him, sir. He sent me to see you. I wish there were something that could be done. I really should be doing better.

PROFESSOR: Well, just try harder on the next test. If you would excuse me now, I must prepare for my next lecture.

Approaching an Amoeba

The professor is all stuck up. The dependent student has splashed anxiety all over him. The authority is vaguely aware that his power is being criticized, but when he lashes out, there is nothing but agreement there. He is punching a bag of yesses.

In such a pseudoencounter, the dependent person is like an amoeba. He is a single-minded animal who always glides toward the source of light, or in this case, toward power. He fits himself into any shape that is necessary to get where he wants to go.

Suppose the professor had been more aware of what formidable obstacles he faced? Then he might have held the light steady, so to speak, until the amoeba was more or less in sight. Then the boundaries of personality could be observed and the motivations clarified.

STUDENT: Sir, I would like to talk to you about my grades. I am not doing as well as I would like to do. I am confused by the tests.

PROFESSOR: How well would you like to do?

STUDENT: Well, ah, I think I should be doing much better. I made all A's in high school. I study long hours and I think that I should do better here.

PROFESSOR: Why?

STUDENT: Well, people have told me that I am a good student. Now, I do not say that for myself, but that is what I have been told and my grades do seem to indicate that. At least in the past that was so. There must be something wrong with the way I am reading the tests now, like the last quiz that you gave.

PROFESSOR: Do you agree with the people who tell you that you are very smart?

STUDENT: Well, I think that I can understand a question if it is on material that we have covered in class. Some of your questions were not on material that we had covered in class.

PROFESSOR: You have never been asked a question on material that was not covered in class?

STUDENT: No, I have not! I really do not think that is fair.

PROFESSOR: Maybe that is one difference between high school and college. In college, we have assigned reading and expect you to be able to answer questions on it, whether we discuss it in class or not.

STUDENT: Well, a lot of us have difficulty with your questions. I would appreciate it if you would spend more time explaining things. It would be a great help. Could you do this for us?

PROFESSOR: I wonder if you have thought of some other ways of understanding the material, besides asking me to explain it to you.

STUDENT: Well, sir, I will be glad to try whatever you might suggest. (Pause.) What would you suggest, sir?

PROFESSOR: I would suggest that you think over my question.

STUDENT: Yes, sir. Now, just which question was that, sir?

PROFESSOR: I want you to think of ways to understand material that is assigned to you, whether it is discussed in class or not. If you come to see me again, I will want to know what answers you have thought of.

STUDENT (*rising abruptly*): Yes, sir. I'll do that.

For today, the game is over. The student has not succeeded in threatening the professor and placing blame for poor performance upon him. The professor has not attacked the student or sought to defend himself. But he has tried to raise the kinds of questions that would help a person to make some independent moves on his own.

Dominant and Passive Dependency

Something seems out of place in these interviews. They are supposed to be conversations with a very dependent person, yet that person makes attacks upon a strong authority and seeks to threaten one in power. In fact, he uses "yes" in a very aggressive way. How can this impetuous movement be reconciled with our picture of a dependent person?

Actually, there should be no confusion. A dependent person may be very aggressive. He is after approval, and he will do whatever is necessary to get it. In fact, some psychologists have defined an extreme group of "yea-sayers." These are students who consistently respond with yes to items on a questionnaire or interview.

The yea-sayer is very voluble. He can speak very easily about himself, although with very little depth. He takes suggestions readily, reacts quickly to the moods of others, makes himself very much at ease with an authority. He is not very stable, however, for he will wander from the subject at hand whenever permitted to do so. The yea-sayer is also very enthusiastic and can impulsively throw himself into any situation that promises a thrill. This is one sign of the shallowness of such a person's reaction. He continually gives a surface response to any question, but he gives it with an enthusiasm that is so appealing.

It is certainly difficult to "pin down" such a person. It is also difficult to be openly annoyed with him. He appears to accept whatever we say, and yet he is continually pushing at us from unexpected angles.

This is the dominant-dependent person of the two interviews. He insinuates what he wants into the conversation. If he finds an opening, he makes an attack. He can withdraw in an instant, so when the student does not get very far in talking about his understanding of the tests, he switches to the complaint that many other students have difficulty with the tests. When this does not work, he appeals to his previous scholastic record, and when that is not enough, he brings up the tradition that every question must first be discussed in class. Here is indeed an elusive opponent! Although the professor is annoyed and frustrated, he cannot really express how he feels, for he is blanketed by a smoke screen of yeses. Superficial compliance hides the maneuvering of the student.

The dominant or aggressive dependent is often rejected, and yet he cannot be shoved away. We are made to feel so guilty for our undefined hostility to him that we do not really say "no." Instead, we often give in reluctantly to his demands and hate ourselves and him for it. This only confirms his picture of others as deceitful and further solidifies his self-contempt. He realizes that we did not give ourselves to him freely, but only upon constraint. So he does not really have what he wants. He will be back tomorrow with new demands.

The best answer to this vicious circle is a firm searchlight upon the self. Ask the person exactly what he wants and why. Ask what other conditions will be brought into the picture. Ask him to set the limits of his demands, and then remember what he has said.

Most of all, do not be magnanimous and forgiving. Be fair and clear. Attempts to "understand" or do more than we ought to for another person will be despised. And when we have overextended ourselves, the dependent person will let us down and we will be angry. Then we will have no one to blame but ourselves, for we were the ones who offered so much.

Find where the person's motivation is, and help *him* to build on that basis.

The same approach is necessary for passively dependent people. At first, such advice may seem almost impossible to follow. How will we ever be able to find the true desires of an introverted, shy individual? If we question or prod, the person retreats further in himself like a turtle into his shell. If some answers are coaxed out, they are weighed and carefully considered before expression. The few tentative expressions of selfhood are very indirect and complicated. There is a lack of spontaneity, a constant waiting for somebody else to say something.

If a passive person does begin to express himself, he is continually worried for fear that he is saying too much, that he is taking over the conversation, that he boasted too much about himself. If we ask for clarification of some of his opinions, he tends to feel that he is being criticized and quickly apologizes or reverts to apathy.

I observe that people form quick relationships with the dominant dependent, and then look for ways to get out of the relationship gracefully. With the passive dependent, people take longer to form a friendship, but then seem very happy with this friend who comes forward so shyly. It seems as though the passive person does have a genuine self deep within that he wants very much to protect. If he feels accepted and cared for, he will gradually bring a little bit of himself to the surface. What we then see is usually very likable, but much reassurance is necessary for the person to see himself as we see him. He has repressed his selfhood under so many years to contempt and rejection.

It is most important that a passively dependent person should receive *honest* acceptance. That is, we must give him an open evaluation of what we see in him. When he talks of himself, he will often express a great deal of self-contempt and think that he has made a fool of himself in company. We may reply that he did seem nervous and ill at ease, but that his comments were appropriate and people seemed to like what he had to say.

This honesty is usually appreciated when the passive person has made an obvious mistake. He is usually depressed and full of reproach. We can admit with him that he has made a mistake, but indicate that we do not beat ourselves down as much as he does when we make mistakes. He should be shown that his self-punishment is inappropriate. If he wants to punish himself just for the sake of punishment, that is his business, but the one mistake that we know about does not warrant so great a self-contempt. Sometimes this realistic view may help the person to see that he is not really as responsible for everything as he believes himself to be.

We are really trying to break the hold of parental voices upon this passive person. For years he has thought that he was responsible for every mistake that was made in his world, just as his mother used to tell him that all depended on his conduct and that any failure on his part would bring misery upon the whole family. It is quite startling for such a person to learn that other people do not consider him to be nearly as important as he has been taught to consider himself. His mistakes do not shake the whole world to its foundations. In fact, most people do not pay attention to his mistakes, as he had fancied they would. It may be that mother is not completely correct, or that everyone does not scrutinize his behavior as father once did. Maybe he could live a little bit without being knocked down again.

It is sometimes amusing to see what happens when a passively dependent person finds a new sense of freedom. He can talk about himself spontaneously without being criticized! He can even criticize others in a direct manner without being embarrassed! All this is so new and interesting that the person proceeds to tell others what he thinks about them with great vigor. Sometimes his remarks are quite penetrating and devastating. The formerly passive person now makes statements that cause bold men to tremble.

The amusing part of this is the way that a formerly passive person interprets what has happened. He does not see himself as a bold, penetrating critic. Instead, he still sees himself as he formerly was, a shy and withdrawn individual who only says a few words, and who would never hurt anyone in the process. He is amazed by the devastation that some of his newfound freedom can bring. "What," one exclaimed to me, "do you mean that *I* made Mr. C. and his salesman anxious?" It was such a delicious, new thought. The problem now is to get the person to see what strength he does have, and to help him take responsibility for what he says and does. This is one part of the question of ethics that we must consider in the next chapter.

Chapter 6

The Deadly Sins of Dependency

A dependent personality pattern may seem to be the safest haven from the alarms of this world. But for reasons beyond my understanding, a self surrendered to anything less than God is miserable. Self-contempt, sloth, envy, jealousy, self-deception, and dogmatism lurk in the haven of rest. An empty soul is a sure meeting place for deadly sins.

Sloth and Despair

A chronically dependent person is continually preyed upon by self-contempt. He tries and tries, but he never seems to make a success of anything. Each new attempt will eventually confirm his self-defeat.

A young lawyer described this process in a thirty-five-year-old man who sought counsel when charged with housebreaking. The client was well oriented, cooperative, and friendly. He was good looking and well developed. He explained that he was charged with breaking into a relative's house while the relative and family were in another state. He said that he was almost drunk at the time and does not remember anything. The client, whom we will call Mr. H., described his family life as very stable. He had a good behavior record in high school, although he did admit that he "caused a little trouble at home." When he left home to join the Army: "things never went right." He received a dishonorable discharge and returned home. His mother died soon after his return and the son began periodic drinking. His father was enraged and would have nothing to do with his delinquent offspring. The young man's brothers and sisters also refused to see him.

Mr. H. decided that he would live up to all the expectations that his father had once had of him. So he tried a job in the same type of business that had brought success to his father. He was not well prepared for his work, was accused of carelessness and had a poor work record, and quit after a minor argument with his boss.

A marriage seemed to be a good way to "settle down." This did seem to make some impression on his father, who now found a position for the son in his own company. The marriage "rocked along" until the birth of a second child, when the wife divorced Mr. H.

Mr. H. did not take his work very seriously and began to pass bad checks to make up for his loss of sales commissions. His father's influence kept him with the company for several years. The father also "made good" all of the bad checks.

But now things seem to be "closing in" on Mr. H. He is "in real trouble with the law." He feels that he has deeply disappointed his father, who is "an upstanding man who wanted all of his children to do good." Mr. H. feels that his father is right in rejecting him because he is "no good."

A similar opinion is expressed about his rejection by his wife, and by friends and relatives. His relationships seem to go in a self-defeating circle. He makes a good first impression, is eager to please, and wins the confidence of people. He then coasts through marriage or a job for several months, becomes bored and begins delinquent behavior.

The delinquency does not seem to be related to any breach of faith on the part of those who trust the client. Instead, Mr. H. deliberately deceives those who have faith in him. His rationale is that people would find out about him sooner or later, and then it would be "no good" for him. He really does not seem capable of believing that others believe in him.

The young lawyer could think of no reasonable way to help his client as a person. He concluded that Mr. H. "always managed to get himself behind the eight ball and stay there."

This is a full-blown case of self-contempt. Mr. H. has accepted himself as an inadequate person and has drifted with this image for years. If he had made major attempts to correct his self-image, then his history might have been different. But he has that combination of self-contempt and drifting that is called sloth, and it is deadly.

Envy and Jealousy

Some dependent persons will drift with any image of themselves. But others are aroused by the picture of themselves as inadequate individuals. They have strong feelings about the way that other people treat them, or evaluate them. They are aware of the contrast between themselves and others, and they do not like what they see.

This conflict can lead a person out of sloth into salvation. Poets, preachers, and novelists have continually provided examples of renewal and character among those who seemed inferior. In George Bernard Shaw's *Pygmalion* the aristocratic Henry Higgins believes that he is only proving a theory about language when he offers speech training to a cockney flower girl, Eliza Doolittle. But Eliza becomes a person of taste and refinement who is emotionally superior to her teacher. She will not accept his image of her as an inferior being.

In the play's musical adaptation, *My Fair Lady,* Eliza Doolittle expresses her fury at the treatment she is receiving from Henry Higgins. Out of that bursts a new self and a new way of speaking.

Tragically, there are many dependent persons who never burst *out.* They just fume within. Instead of new life, there is hopeless envy and recurring jealousy of those who seem more adequate and find many rewards in life. These perils of the soul result from the double-mindedness of the dependent individual. On the one hand, he finds security in his submissive manner of life. On the other hand, he wants to be respected and rewarded as a self-actualized person. He knows what he would like to have, but he is unwilling to take the risks that are necessary to win approval as an independent person.

I have tried on occasion to help some people be content with their dependent pattern of living. It seems to be a very satisfying way of life as I look at it from the outside. But dependent people have taught me that it is a very uncomfortable life that they lead. Furthermore, they resent any open characterization of themselves as less than adequate. They are either unwilling to accept what they have said about themselves as dependent individuals, or feel sure that they are now doing better than they had previously thought of themselves.

Neither culture nor family prepares a middle-class American for openly accepted dependency. It is a label that no one likes to live with.

Concealment

Since the dependent designation is so unacceptable, people argue themselves out of an unfavorable position. The reasoning sometimes goes like this. The troubled person says that he is inadequate. He often feels that he is wrong about things. He is sure that others are more adequate to judge how he should behave than he is. He feels guilty of many sins.

If I make the mistake of impulsively stating that this shows he is very dependent, the individual will agree, but not really agree. He will say that he is bothered about his dependency, and yet he does not know what else he can do. He is a member of a very important group of people, and he wants to agree with them. Some of them have great intelligence and made important decisions that he knows to be right. Why should he disagree with them? Being accepted by the right people is certainly as important as making the right decisions at all times, especially when he knows that some people have more experience and power than he has.

When I ask if there is ever a time when he can stand apart from the group, the defensively dependent person will answer that he certainly could if he wished to do so. But then, he does not want to disrupt the group fellowship. Or if he has ventured a contrary opinion and others do not immediately agree, he drops the point to avoid argument. He is sure that he is right in his opinion, but he does not want to disturb people who cannot see what he sees.

So I am defeated. I have not realized how some dependent persons can complain about their inadequacies and then conceal all their self-surrender. But they do it so well that I am soon to feel unreasonable and unsympathetic. When I begin to feel guilty, then I know that the dependent person has got me. It is time to admit defeat and allow the person to enjoy his triumph over a powerful and successful person.

Of course, when I admit defeat, the victory seems hollow. The deceitfully dependent person is very good at playing games, and is unaccustomed to open expressions of helplessness from those whom he envies. But sometimes he is impressed enough by this to begin to be honest with himself.

Honesty is the best answer to concealment. Along with honesty there must come self-surrender. This sounds curious to suggest, for dependent people already seem to be selling their souls everywhere for approval. What I am suggesting is that they let go of the defensive self-image that they have erected or that others have taught them. It is a challenge for them to lay aside their armor and risk life without excuse.

This does not mean that the dependent person will live without limitations. In previous chapters, I have sought to show how many limitations there are in life and how we must be interdependent. I would especially offer a caution for persons who suffer an orthopedic disability, a spastic paralysis, a cardiac disease, epilepsy, or any other "crippling" disease. These handicaps are real and are not the fantasy of imagination. My concern is with the *self*-concept of handicapped people.

As a matter of fact, persons with physical handicaps adjust much better than many persons would expect them to. In his study of the *Physically Handicapped Woman,* Dr. Carney Landis found that handicapped persons did not tend to be aggressive, irritable, or full of self-pity. They were frustrated more than many others in childhood because they could not have many activities, and as adults they did not express as much interest in others or feeling about themselves as a result of these restrictions. They were less lively, but their lives were not distorted by gross amounts of frustration, annoyance, or hopelessness. They exhibited a normal amount of independence in all areas except those affected by their physical disability.

These conclusions certainly are devastating to dependent persons who use a handicap as a way of extracting favor from others. An inadequate or immature person who uses a physical liability as a means of manipulating others is a devious manipulator, who conceals his real desires behind some obvious malady.

This is a deadly game in which the deceiving dependent is always the loser. He takes the best emotions of others—pity, charity, patience—and uses them to satisfy his own self-esteem.

For example, a man who suffered from a chronic disease was trying to pin the blame for some failures in his work upon a friend. When the friend pointed out the inadequacies of the argument, the man said, "Oh, but if you had suffered as I have suffered, you would never say things like that to me." The friend shook his head and said nothing more. Who would want to continue a discussion with a man who appealed to his handicap as a means of winning an argument?

The "handicapped" person would reply that "anything is fair in love and war." So far as he is concerned, he is at war with the world. People have tried to "do him in" and he is going to fight back. Basically, the person is saying that he is inadequate to face life as he perceives it. In childhood, he probably did not receive the support and affection that was needed at a time when he was very dependent. In adolescence and young adulthood, he might not have found trustworthy persons with whom he could identify. Or if he did identify with some people, they may have exploited him, or he may have exploited them.

In one way or another, he has reached adulthood with a hostile and hopeless view of the world. It is a hopeless world because the person feels that he is inadequate to make things better in the future. It all looks very dark. All he can do is cling to the present and hope that there will not be too much deterioration.

Such a person is like the Jewish doctor in Antwerp who met some of his old friends after the Nazi defeat. When an unthinking acquaintance asked, "What did you do during the war, doctor?" the Jewish physician replied, "I survived."

Dogmatism

For some, survival is made sure through trust in absolute authority. The dependent person will characteristically feel helpless and overevaluate the strength of other individuals. By blind faith in a stronger person, he will hope to find security. Undivided affection and esteem may be expressed for a mate, a relative, a teacher, a pastor, a politician, or a party.

To maintain security, a dogmatic mind must close against all opinions that would contradict the chosen authority. Any number of facts may be presented to change an opinion, but a dogmatic person will not be moved. He is not sure enough of himself to make an independent decision. He can only wait for the authority to tell him what is right and wrong.

Amazing contradictions appear in such people. Major opinions are isolated from one another. A dogmatic individual may hold to half a dozen beliefs, none of which are consistent with each other. And he may change one or more of these at will. Nothing else is disturbed.

His mind is like a flower. The petals can be twisted and rearranged, but his inner security is undisturbed as long as each idea holds to the central stem of absolute authority. Whatever the authority says to believe, he believes.

Other people are accepted or rejected according to their agreement or disagreement with the authoritative person or party. This is a very necessary part of the defense system of some dependent persons. A stranger is considered to be an enemy until he can be identified with some friendly authority. Once the friendly relationship of the stranger to an authority is established, then the dogmatic person will accept almost anything that the approved stranger has to say. There is no discrimination in his acceptance, once the stranger is brought within the safe circle of dogmatism.

Fearful people usually have a set of test questions to know who is to be accepted or rejected. A person may be asked for his "stand" on certain political issues. If he gives acceptable answers, he is then considered secure. Sometimes there are religious test questions by which dogmatic individuals decide for or against the opinion of those who speak to them.

There also are geographical test questions. For example, I spoke to a group of college students in a southern university about the changing patterns of social life in the South. Several students were very annoyed at my "liberal" attitude and asked for verification of some of my statements. When I was able to satisfy most of their questions, one student said with a note of finality, "Well, I have one final question, Where were you born?" When I replied, "North Carolina," he said, "Oh," and sat down.

It was too easy a victory. If the student had not been so dependent upon birthplace, he might have asked where I was educated. Then I would have lost all my standing with him by disclosing my educational development in Washington, D.C. But being a very dependent soul, he never thought of asking another question. How could he argue with another southerner?

The deadliness of dogmatism is twofold. First, the dependent person who embraces this security of a closed mind will not be an individual. He has become a puppet in the hands of stronger people. Secondly, he does not treat others as individuals, but accepts or rejects them according to a stereotyped system of thought or relationships. It is a dehumanized world for all concerned.

Smother Love

It is possible for a dependent person to choose a way of thinking that depersonalizes others. It is equally possible for others to depersonalize him. This depersonalization is both a cause and an effect of chronic dependency.

One cause of depersonalization is maternal overprotection. This is the way that Dr. David Levy described the malady of some children who were either uncontrollable or completely compliant (maternal overprotection). As he looked at these children, he found that they had four major complaints. First, there was excessive contact with the mother. As one boy said, "Mother is always there." She was an omnipresent parent. Nothing could be done without her approval, reaction, or comment.

Second, there was infantilization. Children complained, "Mother still treats me like a baby." Mother might walk a fifth-grader to school, or she might go to the school several times during the day to see if he or she were being ill treated. Or mother might call up a teacher and "bless her out" for discriminating against her child who was given a low grade. Mother protected the child against any fights with children of similar size in the neighborhood, led him across neighbors' yards, dressed him or her with excessive care.

Third, there was a prevention of independent behavior. The children complained that mothers would not let them grow up, would not let them take any risk. If a child tried to climb a tree in the backyard, mother got a ladder and went up to bring down her baby. The baby might be ten or twelve years of age. If a twelve-year-old wanted to go to a camp for children of his age, mother would be in a panic at the very thought of her baby being off in the wilds. What would he do? How would other people know to care for him? Would his food be good? The thought of separation was prohibitive.

Fourth, there was a lack or excess of mature control. The mother either allowed the child to do exactly as he pleased or controlled his every action. So the overprotected child might be either the "best" behaved or "worst" behaved member of a class. One might sit placidly waiting for all instructions, just as he or she did at home. Another would constantly misbehave and bid for attention, which had been his characteristic pattern from the cradle.

These children were suffering from smother love. Their independence was literally overpowered by a maternal person. Dr. Levy found that the mothers were themselves overpowered by maternal instincts. They were women who were "naturally maternal," who had been distressed by many problems about parenthood. Some of them had to accept premature responsibility for a home as children. Others had contracted unsatisfactory marriages and looked for fulfillment in a child. Many of them had suffered long periods of sterility and had fantasied motherhood as the great fulfillment of their life. In some cases a child was born with difficulty, and in other cases there were severe illnesses that threatened the child's life in his first years. It seemed that a natural desire for maternity, plus threats to it, combined to produce an overpowering parent.

In contrast, fathers were submissive, stable individuals, who were usually obedient children of domineering parents.

Fathers and children showed much improvement when they received some professional care. The care for the father usually consisted of one or two talks in which he was encouraged to take more responsibility as a father for his child.

The treatment for the child was of three types. First, there was some separation from the mother, either through boarding school or camp. This was greeted with great relief and growth by most of the children. Secondly, there was specific advice given by the doctor to the child, and some demonstrations of a better way of home relationships when a social worker visited with the family. Thirdly, there was some psychotherapy. Dr. Levy concluded that this was the least valuable means of treatment for these children.

The Extractors

The cases of Dr. Levy show that there is real hope for dependent children who can find an alternative to a domineering parent. The tragedy is that many persons develop a submissive way of life and are preyed upon by other people to perpetuate it.

Our greatest temptation is with the dominant dependent. He is the person who is a yea-sayer. He immediately agrees with almost anything that will win acceptance for him. If he is accepted, he would do almost anything to keep that acceptance. What talents he has can be exploited to the limit by manipulative persons.

A businessman explained the sin and tragedy of extraction in this way. He observed that the personnel department of many companies in his line would hire bright and aggressive young men for attractive salaries. For ten years they would take everything they could out of the growing person's life. He would work long hours, think up new ideas, sell himself and his company with great energy.

When he had spent himself, he would be told that he was slowing down too much to stay with a growing business. The forty-year-old man would then resign or accept a less remunerative position in some branch office.

Then the men had time to think about their last ten years. What had happened? As many modern novelists and sociologists have said, they were given "the royal treatment" to begin with. They were shown the best club and introduced to the most powerful people. Then they were allowed to compete with other men of similar age and talent for a favored position. As long as they did what the company wanted them to do, they thought they had a chance for advancement. But when they were physically and emotionally depleted, they found that others advanced over them.

These young men fit the "marketing" personality as described by Erich Fromm. They sell themselves for a price. They buy relationships. The currency may be money, status, love, approval, security. It is a day-to-day operation, each person getting what he can for himself.

It would seem that the marketing personality is getting what he deserves. Perhaps he is, but there is also an ethical issue for those who lead him along for their own benefit. They have exploited the weaknesses of others for gain, even though they have satisfied the temporary need of the people who depend on them.

A dominant dependent person is as much of an ethical threat to others as he is to himself. He sells his soul to the highest bidder. And what do we then say of the man who buys and sells souls? It takes real surrender to a higher power for astute and adequate persons to see how they could use others, and yet refrain from it.

Chapter 7

Godly and Ungodly Trust

Dependence upon God is an ethical and emotional bulwark for both the strong and the weak. The adequate and observant person who is tempted to dominate the dependent has need for a restraining power beyond himself. He is tempted to treat people as less than persons.

The dependent person needs the sustaining power of religion to *be* a person. He is continually tempted to submerge his individuality in the security of conformity.

Whether a person is strong or weak in personality, his need for a power beyond himself is dramatized in days of trouble. Illness and misfortune magnify the need for succorance. An attitude of dependence upon God may make a person secure enough to lean upon others as well. Religion can also balance dependent and independent needs in time of stress. A dying man can think about the way in which he dies and consider the relationships that are important for him to strengthen or restructure. At least, it happened that way in the case presented in Chapter 3.

I do not wish to claim more for religion than the evidence will support. "Religion" is a most general term that may not differentiate behavior at all. For example, Chaplain Carl Nighswonger and a psychiatrist at the University of Chicago found almost the same attitudes toward death among terminally ill patients who were and who were not church members. We cannot tell very much about religion from surface details such as church membership or questionnaire statements that a person believes in God.

Pro-Religion and Prejudice

It is especially important to distinguish between types of religious orientation when we are talking about dependent people. Gordon Allport has demonstrated this in his studies of religion and prejudice. He found one group of churchgoers who were "indiscriminately pro-religious." They were like the yea-sayers described in a previous chapter as the dominant dependents. These are persons who anxiously say yes to any question that will help them to appear "right" with religion.

The yea-sayer uses religion to provide security, comfort, status, or social support for himself. It is not a value in its own right; it is a tool that serves his dependent needs.

Indiscriminately religious persons scored highest on a test for prejudice. This is consistent with their anxieties. They want to be very close to the accepted group and to avoid any association with people who are thought to be unacceptable. Friendly feelings about Negroes, Mexicans, or Indians would certainly not increase their social status. They are as contemptuous of those on the outskirts of society as they are of themselves as inadequate individuals.

Dr. Allport calls these indiscriminate religionists because they say yes to any kind of religious question, whether it is designed to measure the useful social comfort of religion, or the deeper personal values of religion. They have the dogmatic mind described by Professor Rokeach. Anxiety to conform has obliterated their ability to distinguish different kinds of religious gratification.

Another group of persons made some significant distinctions between types of religion. Dr. Allport quoted one clergyman who said:

Some people come to church to thank God, to acknowledge His glory and to ask His guidance. . . . Others come for what they can get. Their interest in the church is to run it or exploit it rather than to serve it.[11]

Persons who make this distinction are oriented toward a living religion. The service of God is their master motive. They are his servants and reject the use of religion for their own sake or safety. This inner religion is called "intrinsic." People who have this religious orientation score much lower in prejudice than either nominal churchgoers or those who report no church attendance at all. They have found a security that allows them to associate with, and show concern for, the outcasts of society. With a firm and satisfying religious belief, they are freed from much of the dogmatism and authoritarianism that plagues the nominal church attender.

It is true, therefore, that religion does make a difference, but first we must label the different kinds of religion.

Absolute and Relative Dependence

There also needs to be some discrimination between types of dependence. The eighteenth-century German theologian Friedrich Schleiermacher provided the classic distinction in *The Christian Faith*. He described two elements in our self-consciousness, a relative freedom or dependence and a feeling of absolute dependence.

Relative dependence is our awareness that we can make *some* choices of our own. Independent decisions are possible within certain limitations. Our freedom of choice is related to the world in which we live. Within the world of the family and society we can become a self.

Absolute dependence is a feeling that we are part of a larger unity than our family or our society. We are essentially creatures of God. He has made us and we are his own. We find by experience that we are moral beings, that our choices are related to something beyond ourselves. Experience teaches us that we must go beyond the human relationships, that matter so much, to some Power which has bound the whole of relationships together.

Most of the topics in this book would fall under the classification of "relative" dependence. We have identified the influences of culture and family upon the self. We have explored the self-consciousness of dependent people.

Schleiermacher does not make a complete separation between relative and absolute dependence. The feeling of absolute dependence can provide a necessary balance to some of the types of dependence that we have seen.

First, absolute dependence is a feeling of unified personal existence. We are aware that God has created us for himself, and that we are more dependent upon him as creator than we are upon any group of people who have sustained us as creatures. The primacy of our loyalty is established toward God, and in this loyalty we find personal fulfillment. Duty to God comes before love for man.

Second, this consciousness of ourself before God enables us to rise above the people and places who are so important to us in this world. We know that we live in this world and are *partially* dependent upon it, but our absolute dependence is upon a power that moves all of us. Even the most powerful beings around us are subject to God, someday, some way.

This means freedom from the past and hope for the future. Even the most dependent personality can find meaning in the experience of a place of worth before God. Trust in him is the ground of hope.

Third, the feeling of absolute dependence is just what it says, a feeling. It is a reality in our experience, in the awareness of our selfhood. It is the intrinsic religion described by Gordon Allport, an awareness that we live for a being beyond ourselves. Although there certainly are philosophical ways of talking about this experience, absolute dependence is not just an idea. A high level of intelligence or a wide degree of experience is not necessary for someone to feel that he belongs to God. Persons with severe personal limitations, intellectual, emotional, physical, can be aware that they belong to their creator.

Fourth, the feeling of absolute dependence is always related to this world. It is the relative dependencies of family and society that give us part of the personal awareness of God. Schleiermacher made this relationship dramatic in his charming dialogue between persons on *The Christmas Eve.* In the Christmas story, God the creator enters time and space as Christ, the Savior. There is a specific time and a concrete event. Men can now think about God in terms of their own experiences with the family. Childhood, motherhood, fatherhood, are self-experiences that now come close to Saviorhood. The babe who was born in a manger was relatively dependent upon man, but he has come to demonstrate absolute dependence upon God.

Being Before Doing

The experience of absolute dependence can be especially helpful to people who seem "absolutely" dependent upon others. Persons who are immobilized by birth defects or chronic disease are not able to do anything for themselves in the normal sense of that phrase. Similarly, there are neurotic and psychotic experiences that paralyze the productivity of a person. As we have asked a number of times before, can a person have self-esteem when he only exists? Can he be anything without doing anything?

The experience of absolute dependence would place being before doing. We are someone when we recognize our dependence upon God, our creator. What we do in this life will depend upon the degree of freedom that our body, talents, or opportunities allow. If we are so severely restricted that we have no opportunities for work, this will not detract from our ultimate significance as persons.

All that really matters is our willingness to praise God for his creation. Such an attitude will mean quite a revolution in the "being" of some people. It will be a turning from a passive to a productive view of life. Instead of asking what can life contribute to me, or what can I get out of life, the major question will be, what can I contribute to life?

A Vienna psychiatrist, Dr. Viktor Frankl, has called the process of this turning, "logotherapy." It is a movement toward meaning beyond oneself. It is "Daseinsanalysis," the understanding of being.

Dr. Frankl came to this understanding in a Nazi prison camp. If ever man had devised a way to make other men less than human, it would be in such a place. Nothing done by a prisoner was praised or considered productive in the Aryan society. Jews and political prisoners were given only enough to sustain their animal labor for a short period of time.

In the midst of this depressing depravity, Dr. Frankl was sustained by thoughts of his wife, and their happiness together. He also thought of a book which would describe the new experience of being that was emerging in prison. He found hope for the future in the maintenance of a productive inner life for the present. There was nothing he could *do* that was right, but there were attitudes he could hold in himself that gave hope for the present and promise for another day.

A part of Dr. Frankl's psychic salvation was his acceptance of complete physical dependency for the time being. This kind of acceptance can bring serenity to people who would weary themselves needlessly in chafing under a cast, resisting bed rest, or trying to persuade attendants to let them out of a mental hospital *today*.

This will certainly be a difficult struggle, for psycho-therapists have found that dependent individuals with a high need for approval quit therapy much earlier than more independent patients. As Chapter 6 has shown, the defensively dependent person cannot stand to be openly treated as one who must have approval from others. Deep within himself he feels so unworthy that he expects complete rejection when people find out what he is really like.

What absolute dependence tries to teach is that we all need a strength beyond ourselves. We were created that way. It is no loss of face to accept ourselves as human. What we need is courage to depend upon God in spite of our fears that honesty and self-revelation would lead to rejection and meaninglessness.

An acceptance of meaning in spite of dependence is the re-creation of self-esteem. For some mental hospital patients, it means the acceptance of responsibility for some of the suffering that has led to their mental collapse. When such a person is willing to say, "Well, this is the kind of person I *am*, and I must shoulder some of the responsibility for being this way," then the person can cooperate realistically with therapists toward recovery. Prof. Melvin Kimble, of Northwestern Lutheran Theological Seminary, found one woman in a mental hospital who had suffered any number of rejections from others. But as she talked about her hurt and grief with the chaplain, she began to see that her reaction to the betrayal by others was as significant for her present state as the betrayal event itself. Or, as she put it, "There is nothing I can do about the way some men treated me, but I can do something about my attitudes toward men in general." She did not have to distrust all men because her husband and father had been untrustworthy. She certainly had reason for her present distrust, but it was up to her to decide whether she would build the rest of her life around trust or distrust.

Here is the balance between independence and dependence. The lady recognized that she was where she was in part because of what other people had made her to be. This was an acceptance of dependence. But it was a relative dependence, an uneasy, temporary surrender to the past. She was unwilling for it to be absolute. Instead, with skillful help, she was able to become what she ought to be by accepting some responsibility for past, present, and future. What she could be now became more hopeful than what she had been.

A person must go through a good deal of suffering to reach this hopeful point. This takes courage to hope for something better in ourselves than we have known before. It is a call for a more independent life that is sustained by a power beyond our present experiences.

Institutional Dependence

It would be good to think that people could readily reach independence through religion. But the evidence is not so hopeful. There are a number of studies that show excessively dependent people gravitating toward the church as an institution. Those who feel inadequate are most likely to accept authoritarianism—religious, political, or regional.

Instead of the absolute dependence of religion leading toward more independence of family and society, there are many instances in which dependence upon God has been used to maintain dependence upon men. The absolute has become a part of the relative. The religious institution has become the blender of two into one.

An example of this institutionalized religion is the study of rural youth by Dr. Leo Rippy, of Scarritt College. Dr. Rippy found that the most faithful attenders of youth groups were passive, withdrawn, and dependent young people. These young persons scored high on tests of endurance, self-severity, and a sense of closeness to God and family. They came to the Sunday evening programs and they studied their lessons for such programs.

More vigorous young persons were seldom seen at youth programs after early adolescence. If they did attend, they took little interest and seldom studied the prescribed lessons. But this was no sign of lessening religious interest on the part of the more independently-minded young persons. They continued to show a consistently high level of attendance at worship services in the morning.

In discussing these findings with the Religious Research Association in 1966, Dr. Rippy thought that adult leadership was one factor in the significant dropout of independent youth. He found that adults usually did not know the young people of the church well, and imposed an authoritarian pattern upon those who did attend youth services. If the adult leadership were more independently minded, they might develop programs that would attract the youth leaders who were now going elsewhere on Sunday evening.

But to follow this suggestion would be to magnify the difference between absolute and relative dependence. It would mean that the worship of God would throw family and society into a lesser place. Questions would be raised about the customs of a region, the sanctity of segregation, and rural mores. The foundations of cultural religion might be shaken.

Persons who have looked to religion as the repository of the *status quo* could not stand such an awakening. In fact, these swift changes of modern society compel many to seek a religion that upholds the old-time virtues. By this, they do not mean the virtue of absolute dependence upon God and the development of character that will stand for integrity amid the changing fashion of the time. What they desire is a mixture of this ideal with the small-town or neighborhood customs of their childhood. They want a religion of reassurance, a nostalgic return to home. They desire conformity to a tradition rather than transformation of self and society.

Transforming a Tradition

How can religion be changed from an institutionalized refuge for the *status quo* into a dynamic force for the transformation of men and movements? With particular respect to the dependent personality and the dependent needs of all people, I can offer several suggestions.

First, we need to accept religion as a social and emotional refuge for people who are harried and handicapped in society. Churches and synagogues can be "cities of refuge," even as they were in the Old Testament. Men who fled for their lives in those ancient days could find sanctuary in specific cities of Israel. Here they would be safe from avengers if they had accidentally caused the death of another.

There are times when all of us are fleeing from something, and we need a safe refuge. If we can accept our own dependent needs, then we may accept religion as a refuge.

Second, we need to accept religion as a *permanent* source of emotional, social, and ideological security for some people. Pure and undefiled religion is not for this purpose, but this is the way it is used by some very inadequate individuals. These are the fearful persons who must absolutize all authority, who make religion and culture one, who insist that people are accepted or rejected on the basis of rigid dogma, whether it be economic, theological, or social.

These persons cannot be torn loose from the only moorings they have found for the self. I would let them have a place in a religious establishment, but I certainly would not allow them to dominate it. Religious institutions should be led by those who know the difference between absolute and relative dependence, and who have experienced the transforming power of an absolute in their own lives. I would not argue or seek to change those who are authoritarian in religion. I would only state that I do not see religion as they do and do not know of any way that would lead them to agree with me. I would not want them to prosper, but I certainly would not pursue them.

Third, I would respect the necessity of anchoring points for any personal or social change. It is necessary, as we saw in Chapters 1 and 2, for people to know the facts and identify the sources before they will willingly move in a different direction. So if religion is to be a force for change, it must identify the beliefs necessary for movement in a new direction. There are usually a great variety of theological sources for new directions in society. For example, I detect different reasons for civil rights among northern and southern Christians. White Protestant church leaders in the North have emphasized God as the creator of all men. This has been the theological rationale for their equality campaigns. The brotherhood of man has been a natural extension of this doctrine. In the South, the emphasis has been upon God as Savior through Christ. Men are considered worthy because Jesus has died for them. Men are to be treated as equal because they are all worthy through redemption in Christ. Furthermore, men will not be saved unless they are treated as brothers by Christians.

The movement toward equality and civil rights is spurred on by different theological traditions in various parts of the country. The principle I press for is a recognition that some definable doctrine must anchor any movement for social or personal change. There is no one doctrine that will always do this, but there must be a doctrine for people to feel secure enough to let go of what they now have. We must present them with a hope and a challenge beyond themselves. But it must be a challenge that is based upon a commitment that they have already made.

Fourth, religion can keep the balance between dependent and independent needs. Studies of the pastoral office have shown two traditions, one of comfort and the other of challenge. The first of these has been the ministry to the sick, the care of the dying, the instruction of children, the guidance of the weak, and the restraint of the tempted. It is a sustaining, guiding force of the spirit.

The other tradition is disciplinary. It is a call for people to change, to learn a better way of life, to cease and desist from wicked ways.

On the American frontier, church discipline was a restraint against conformity to "the world," or personal temptations of "the flesh." A person was challenged to be a worthy person, he was restrained from descent into attitudes or behavior that were less than the best in a human being.

And this occurred in a culture that was new, fresh, and changing. It was based on a dependence upon God and an interdependence with a fellowship of believers. In some cases, this was strong enough to create a new and fresh society. It gives hope that men can find some dependable anchorage in life that will not only sustain them but also give them strength and vision for the transformation of a shifting society.

Chapter 8

Creative Insecurity

When we know that we need people, and have that need met in healthy ways, we can be creative people. We can stand on some firm foundations while we cut new channels for living. We do not need to grasp every straw of security. Much of the chaff of life can drift by. We can make distinctions between that which perishes and that which persists.

This kind of creativity is stimulated by the knowledge of our insecurity. That is, we know our limitations. There are uncertainties in life, and we must be prepared for them. We will not be ready unless we take seriously the place of dependency in ourselves and our world.

Dependency is a pointer toward some neglected parts of modern life. First, our modern world neglects the inner self. There are so many rewards for ambitious people, so much success for the self-made man. We have not looked closely at our need for love, affection, approval. This is a necessary dimension of life, without which our self will die. We saw two examples of this in the previous chapter. A bitter woman in a mental hospital finally admitted that she had to depend on some men. She could not distrust mankind and be a well person. This was the beginning of her recovery. Secondly, there was the inner life of Dr.

Frankl who could think of himself as a loving and productive person in the midst of Nazi depravity.

A second neglected dimension is evil. We seldom think of natural evil because we are so sure that modern science will conquer sickness and disaster. Technical advances have certainly increased our life-span. But every city newspaper has accounts of accidental deaths every day. We are often shocked to hear of tragedy that comes to a friend or acquaintance. Why? Could it not be us? John Donne wrote in a quieter century that no man was an island to himself. We all suffer the same fate. When the bell tolls in the parish churchyard, why send a servant to learn who has died? The bell is a reminder that we all die.

This dimension of dependency does not need to be morbid. It can be a healthy reminder to enjoy each day in a godly way. What values are really worth living for if we have but a few hours? An early Puritan, Samuel Sewell, thought this way when he heard that a middle-aged acquaintance had died. He "took stock" of his own plans for the coming years and asked what he was storing up against the day of disease and death. When a wealthy merchant can ask himself these serious questions, he can be led to a deeper and more loving life.

Thirdly, dependency adds time and eternity to our world. We are in such a hurry, we obey so many impulses. Much advertising and selling is based on impulse buying. No one is to delay gratification. Everyone is to enjoy *now*.

But sometimes we are trapped like Henry VI. Shakespeare characterizes him as an unhappy king who looks out of a farm-house window upon the dreary War of the Roses about him. Powerful nobles fight each other for a kingdom in ruins. There seems to be no end to bloodshed and cruelty.

The king thinks of the dreary way in which day follows day. When will it end?

Hopefully, we will not need a civil war to see that life stretches beyond the gratification of daily impulses. The person who is independent today will be dependent tomorrow. And if a robust individual thinks that he will die of a sudden heart attack with no trouble to anyone, there is still the question of eternity. What can he depend on in the life beyond death?

Here we are very much in a shadowy region. It is the deepest of all and no one can penetrate it. While we wait to know the future, we can expand our self-awareness in the here and now. How much do we accept and live with our need for others? How responsible are we in balancing this need with some independent decisions?

Time and motion can also be altered today. Does our schedule reflect the values on which we depend? Or do we spend more and more time on things that matter less and less? What are our motions like? Do we move round in a circle, centered only on approval? Or do we launch out in some activities that proclaim our security in values beyond our immediate society?

These are the questions that should create a creative insecurity. They are reminders that there is no hiding place down here. But they are also a challenge to find an anchor.

That anchor is beyond the self. The problem is to see the anchor as it is. Here is where we can connect material from various topics that we have discussed. Our view of ourselves and our view of God are closely related. The dependent persons that we discussed in Chapter 5 are going to see God in a different way from the self-actualized persons mentioned in Chapter 3 and elsewhere.

An inadequate self would surrender to an inadequate God. That is, the constitutionally dependent person would think of himself as a worm or clod who was pushed about by a tyrant in heaven. He would not see God as a loving creator. Consequently, he would not think of religion as creative. It would be only the straitjacket of dogmatism that we have seen in the previous chapter. So we must help people to see themselves differently at the same time that we call them to dependence upon a different kind of authority.

This can lead to a contradiction. The anchor always seems to be changing. World, self, God, are so closely connected that a shift in our understanding of one will bring a shift in our understanding of the other two. There is always some question as to just where the anchor holds. This is the creative insecurity with which we must always live.

Notes

1. *The Washington Post,* May 7, 1967.

2. Thomas Wieser, ed., *Planning for Mission* (U. S. Conference for the World Council of Churches, 1966), p. 196.

3. Erich Fromm, *Man for Himself* (Holt, Rinehart and Winston, Inc., 1947), p. 141.

4. Joseph W. Eaton and Robert J. Weil, *Culture and Mental Disorders* (The Free Press of Glencoe, 1955).

5. Elizabeth Ross, "The Dying Patient as Teacher: An Experiment and an Experience," *The Chicago Theological Seminary Register* (December, 1966), pp. 12–13. © The Chicago Theological Seminary. Reprinted by permission.

6. Herbert Mardis, "The Case of Mrs. H.: A Report of Three Interviews Between Mrs. H. and a Minister," *The Chicago Theological Seminary Register,* Vol. 50, No. 6 (February, 1965), pp. 12–14. © The Chicago Theological Seminary. Reprinted by permission.

7. *Handbook of Clinical Psychology,* ed. by Benjamin B. Wolman, p. 1369.

8. Valerie Goldstein, "The Human Situation: A Feminine Viewpoint," *The Nature of Man,* ed. by Simon Doniger, p. 165.

9. John Bunyan, *The Pilgrim's Progress* (Washington Square Press, Inc., 1957), pp. 74 f.

10. Richard S. Crutchfield, "Conformity and Character," *The American Psychologist*, Vol. 10 (1955), p. 195. Copyright, 1955, by the American Psychological Association, and reproduced by permission.

11. Gordon W. Allport and J. Michael Ross, "Personal Religious Orientation and Prejudice," *Journal of Personality and Social Psychology*, Vol. 5, No. 4, p. 445.